974.5
Hei

DISCARDED

6498

DATE DUE

Metro Litho
Oak Forest, IL 60452

00485-9

974.5   Heinrichs, Ann
HEI   America the beautiful.
             Rhode Island

AMERICA the BEAUTIFUL

RHODE ISLAND

By Ann Heinrichs

Consultants

Rose Marie Cipriano, Principal, Cumberland High School, Cumberland, Rhode Island

Mildred Mosher Chamberlain, Certified Genealogist, Warwick, Rhode Island

Robert L. Hillerich, Ph.D., Bowling Green State University, Bowling Green, Ohio

CHILDRENS PRESS®
CHICAGO

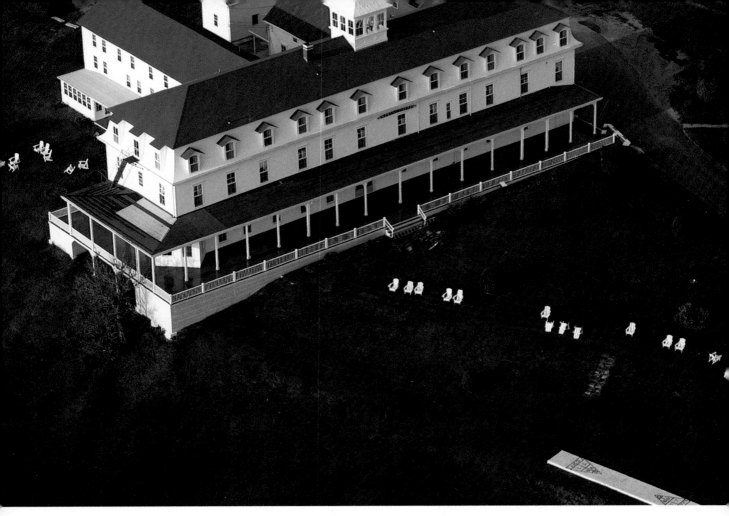

A hotel on Block Island

Project Editor: Joan Downing
Associate Editor: Shari Joffe
Design Director: Margrit Fiddle
Typesetting: Graphic Connections, Inc.
Engraving: Liberty Photoengraving

Copyright © 1990 by Childrens Press®, Inc.
All rights reserved. Published simultaneously in Canada.
Printed in the United States of America.
 2 3 4 5 6 7 8 9 10 R 99 98 97 96 95 94 93 92 91

Library of Congress Cataloging-in-Publication Data

Heinrichs, Ann.
    America the beautiful. Rhode Island / by Ann
Heinrichs.
        p.   cm.
    Includes index.
    Summary: Introduces the geography, history,
government, economy, industry, culture, historic sites,
and famous people of the Ocean State.
    ISBN 0-516-00485-9
    1. Rhode Island—Juvenile literature. [1. Rhode
Island.] I. Title.
F79.3.H45   1990   89-25284
974.5—dc20   CIP
                                         AC

A Providence home owner rehabbing his colonial-period house

TABLE OF CONTENTS

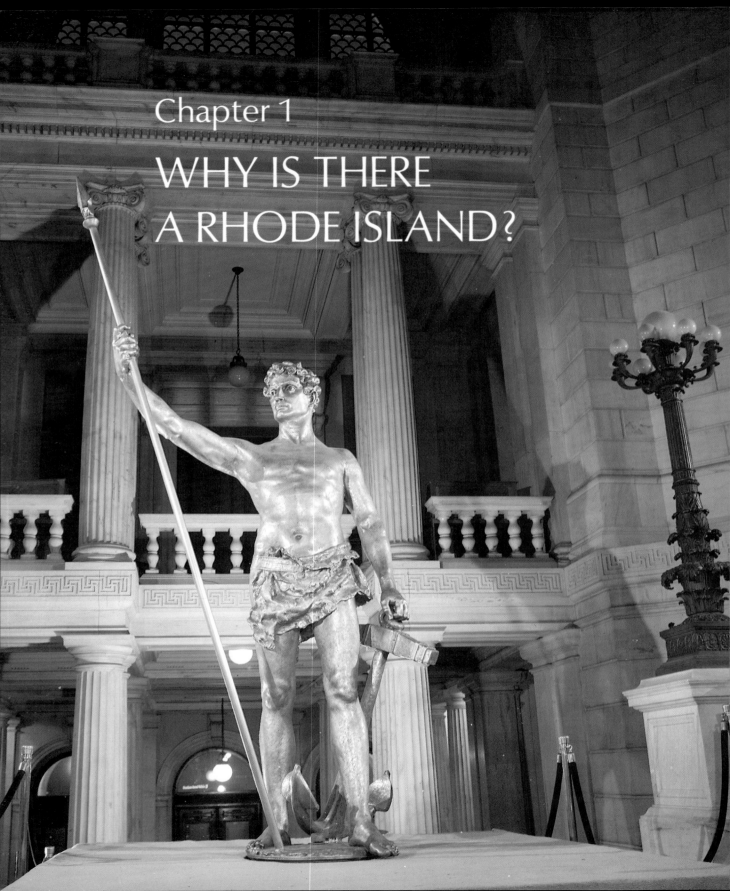

Chapter 1

WHY IS THERE
A RHODE ISLAND?

WHY IS THERE A RHODE ISLAND?

"Why is there a state of Rhode Island?" asked historian Sydney James in the preface of his volume on colonial Rhode Island. In its early days, the troublesome little colony caused its neighbors to utter a similar question.

Unique among America's original thirteen colonies, Rhode Island governed itself and granted its residents religious freedom. Thus it came to be known as the place "where people think otherwise." In a less kindly vein, it was called "Rogue's Island" and "the Sinke into which all the Rest of the Colonyes empty their Hereticks." Yet the very freedoms that invited such ridicule — self governance and religious liberty — later became cornerstones of the United States Constitution.

In the 1800s, a manufacturing boom lured thousands of immigrants to the state's factories and mills: Irish, French-Canadians, Italians, Portuguese, Russians, and many others. These newcomers gave Rhode Island the same ethnic diversity that strengthens and enriches America's social fabric today.

Rhode Islanders point proudly to a number of other distinctions. Rhode Island was the first colony to declare independence from England. It was the birthplace of the United States Navy and the American Industrial Revolution. Its craftspeople make it the jewelry and silverware capital of the world.

Why is there a state of Rhode Island? One could easily answer, "To show the United States what America is all about."

Chapter 2
THE LAND

THE LAND

GEOGRAPHY

Tiny Rhode Island, sometimes affectionately called "Little Rhody," is the smallest of the fifty states. Nearly five hundred Rhode Islands could fit inside Alaska, the nation's largest state. From north to south, Rhode Island's mainland measures only about 48 miles (77 kilometers). Its longest distance from east to west is about 37 miles (60 kilometers). Counting its inland waterways, but not its bay waters, Rhode Island's land area covers 1,214 square miles (3,144 square kilometers).

Situated in the far northeastern United States, Rhode Island belongs—along with Maine, New Hampshire, Vermont, Massachusetts, and Connecticut—to the group of states called New England. Shaped roughly like a long rectangle, Little Rhody fits neatly into a niche between Connecticut, on its western border, and Massachusetts, to the north and east. Narragansett Bay cuts into the southern two-thirds of the state, and the Atlantic Ocean washes Rhode Island's southern shores.

TOPOGRAPHY

The land of Rhode Island is divided into two regions: the Coastal Lowlands and the Eastern New England Upland. The Coastal Lowlands include the southern and eastern part of the mainland, the islands in Narragansett Bay, and the land east of the bay that borders Massachusetts. Miles of sandy beaches and rocky

A salt marsh on Conanicut Island in Narragansett Bay

cliffs line the water's edge in this coastal region. Lagoons and salt
ponds are common along the southern coast, while jagged
promontories jut out from the eastern coast and the islands in the
bay. Farther inland, the coastal flatlands give way to hilly slopes.
The mainland's hills are jagged and forested, while those east of
the bay are gently rounded, with few trees. Rhode Island's
lowlands are part of the coastal lowlands that extend all along the
New England coast.

The inland slopes continue to rise into the Eastern New England
Upland of northern and western Rhode Island. Although the state
has no mountains, the upland hills are higher than those in the
lowlands, rising from 200 feet (61 meters) in the east to over 800
feet (244 meters) in the northwest. At the far western edge of the
state is Jerimoth Hill, the state's highest point, standing 812 feet
(247 meters) above sea level. Nestled in little valleys throughout
the upland are many ponds and lakes.

Although Rhode Island is nicknamed the Ocean State, it is really Narragansett Bay, rather than the Atlantic Ocean, that provides most of the state's shoreline.

ISLANDS

Clustered within Narragansett Bay are thirty-five islands. To the south, and actually lying in the Atlantic Ocean, is a thirty-sixth, Block Island. For early seamen who sailed into Narragansett Bay, these islands were a treacherous challenge. Over the years, hundreds of ships ran aground or smashed into the rocky cliffs along the islands' shores.

Though some of the islands are large and can be sighted easily from a distance, many are small but dangerous clumps of rock. The smallest of the state's islands, fittingly named Despair, is merely a rocky mass in Narragansett Bay. The largest island, covering 45 square miles (117 square kilometers), is Aquidneck Island, officially named the Island of Rhode Island. Block Island, which lies about 10 miles (16 kilometers) south of the mainland, is a popular recreation area with an intriguing historical background. Once a smugglers' hideaway, Block Island was a seaman's nightmare. Close to two hundred major shipwrecks have been recorded on its shores.

WATER, WATER, EVERYWHERE

Although Rhode Island is nicknamed the Ocean State, the Atlantic Ocean washes against only 40 miles (64 kilometers) of its coastline. It is Narragansett Bay, extending 28 miles (45 kilometers) inland, that provides Rhode Island with most of its sandy shoreline. Counting all the coastline along the bay, as well as the shorelines of its islands, Rhode Island can boast a total coastline of 384 miles (618 kilometers).

Once the nation's most industrialized state, Rhode Island powered its factories and mills with the rushing waters of its many rivers. Though most of Rhode Island's inland waters are fresh (nonsalty), in some spots the salt waters of Narragansett Bay reach into the mainland. Greenwich Bay, Mount Hope Bay, and the Sakonnet, Providence, and Seekonk rivers are all saltwater extensions of Narragansett Bay. At their source far upstream, the Seekonk's waters begin as the freshwater Blackstone and flow into the Pawtucket River before reaching the Seekonk.

Freshwater rivers that flow into the salty bay include the Pettaquamscutt, Potowomut, Pawtuxet, and Woonasquatucket rivers. Other important rivers are the Pawcatuck (forming part of Rhode Island's southwest border with Connecticut), Wood, Ponaganset, Chepachet, and Moshassuck rivers. Waterfalls grace many of Rhode Island's rivers as they rush through the countryside's sloping terrain.

Nearly three hundred reservoirs, lakes, and ponds are scattered throughout the state. The largest reservoir, located on the north branch of the Pawtuxet River, is the Scituate Reservoir. With its five tributaries, it holds a total of 41 billion gallons (155 billion liters) of water. Greater Providence draws its water supply from the Scituate. Some of the state's other bodies of water are Watchaug Pond, Worden Pond, and Point Judith Pond.

CLIMATE

With breezes from the Atlantic Ocean and Narragansett Bay moderating Rhode Island's climate, the state rarely experiences severe extremes in temperature. January and February are the coldest months. In January, the temperature averages 29 degrees Fahrenheit (minus 2 degrees Celsius). On January 11, 1942, Kingston registered the state's coldest temperature: minus 23 degrees Fahrenheit (minus 30.5 degrees Celsius).

In July, Rhode Islanders can expect an average temperature of 71 degrees Fahrenheit (22 degrees Celsius). Still, temperatures over 90 degrees Fahrenheit (32 degrees Celsius) occur an average of eight days a year, and summer droughts are not uncommon. July and August are usually the hottest months, as residents of Providence can attest. On August 2, 1975, they suffered the state's highest recorded temperature, 104 degrees Fahrenheit (40 degrees Celsius).

About 44 inches (112 centimeters) of precipitation (rain, snow and other moisture) fall on Rhode Island every year. Of that, about 31 inches (79 centimeters) is snow. Snowstorms follow an unusual pattern in Rhode Island. The same snowstorm has been known to deposit three times as much snow in the northern part of the state as in the south. Also, as coastal breezes collide with snowstorms, they typically change the snow to rain. Summer thunderstorms bring much of Rhode Island's rain.

Winter (left) and fall
(above) in Rhode Island

Late summer and early fall is the season for hurricane watches. Hurricanes, tidal waves, and other coastal storms have ravaged Rhode Island's coast for centuries. The state's most devastating hurricane hit in 1938, with other major weather disasters striking in 1815, 1869, 1944, 1954, 1955, and 1960.

PLANT AND ANIMAL LIFE

With its great variations in climate and topography, Rhode Island is able to support an interesting array of animals and plants. Even though the state is highly industrialized, more than 60 percent of its land is forested. Ashes, oaks, cedars, birches, pines, hickories, beeches, and elms are some of the more common trees. Paper birches, also known as canoe birches from Indian days, are abundant in the northern woods.

Ferns are found almost everywhere, and wildflowers such as violets, asters, goldenrod, and lilies add swatches of color to the

People who love the outdoors can enjoy both ocean and forest in Rhode Island.

countryside. In the woodlands grow such flowering shrubs as rhododendrons, wild roses, mountain laurels, and dogwoods. Cattails sway along the southern coastal marshlands west of Point Judith.

More than fifty species of wild mammals roam Rhode Island's woodlands. The most common are rabbits, squirrels, moles, skunks, beavers, muskrats, foxes, raccoons, mink, and white-tailed deer. As they migrate along the Atlantic Flyway, woodcocks, rails, mourning doves, and many species of geese and ducks stop along Rhode Island's woods and shores. Native blue jays, robins, sparrows, catbirds, and flickers are common in the woodlands. Hawks and barred owls are harder to find, however, and falcons and eagles are in danger of disappearing altogether. Along the shoreline, gulls, terns, loons, and ospreys can be seen diving for their food. Game birds, whose populations are controlled by legal hunting seasons, include pheasant, quail, partridges, woodcocks, and wild ducks.

Nature's bounty in Rhode Island includes many
kinds of flowers (right) and shellfish (above).

Rhode Island's inland and offshore waters abound with fish and
shellfish. Most fish can live in only one kind of water—either
fresh water or salt water. Rhode Island is fortunate to have both
kinds. Freshwater fishermen find pike, bass, perch, eels, pickerel,
and trout. Saltwater species include bluefin tuna, shark, flounder,
swordfish, white marlin, bluefish, butterfish, striped bass, cod,
and menhaden. A wealth of shellfish are found offshore as well,
notably lobsters, oysters, quahogs (hard clams), soft-shell clams,
scallops, crabs, and mussels.

Rhode Island's Department of Environmental Management was
established in 1977. It helps prevent and manage such disasters as
the accidental spilling of 1 million gallons (3.8 million liters) of oil
in the waters off Newport in 1989. Along with other state
agencies, the department makes sure Rhode Island's waters and
other natural resources are kept clean and safe—for both wildlife
and people.

Chapter 3
THE PEOPLE

LITTLE COMPTON
GARDEN CLUB

THE PEOPLE

POPULATION

   Although no other state has a smaller area than Rhode Island,
ten states have smaller populations. With 947,154 people
according to the 1980 census, the state ranks fortieth in
population. An average of 780 Rhode Islanders occupy each
square mile of the state (301 people for each square kilometer).
This makes Rhode Island's population nearly twelve times as
dense as the national average of 67 people per square mile
(26 people per square kilometer).

   About 87 percent of Rhode Islanders live in cities and their
suburbs, while 13 percent live in rural areas. Nearly two-thirds of
Rhode Island's residents live in the Providence metropolitan area.
This heavily commercial and industrial area along the north and
west shores of Narragansett Bay includes the cities and
surrounding suburbs of Providence, Pawtucket, and Warwick.
Other large population centers are Cranston, East Providence,
Woonsocket, and Newport.

   Eight communities in Rhode Island are officially called "cities,"
and thirty-one others are designated as "towns." The cities, in
descending order of population, are Providence, Warwick,
Cranston, Pawtucket, East Providence, Woonsocket, Newport, and
Central Falls. Not all the cities are larger than the towns, however.
Ten towns have larger populations than Central Falls, which is
the smallest city.

The capital city of Providence is Rhode Island's most-populous city.

Rhode Island's population grew steadily in the 1800s as immigrants poured in to work in the state's factories and mills. This trend slowed in the 1920s as immigration quotas were imposed and the textile industry declined. Between 1970 and 1980, for the first time in its history, the state showed a slight drop in population. By 1985, however, the census bureau estimated the population to have risen to about 968,000.

ETHNIC MIX

Rhode Island has been called the most ethnic state in the nation. Although 90 percent of present-day Rhode Islanders were born in the United States, their backgrounds are a kaleidoscope of ethnic diversity.

The Narragansett Indians are among the ethnic groups whose cultures are celebrated during Providence's annual Heritage Festival on the State House lawn.

About two thousand people in Rhode Island are descended from the region's Native Americans. Most of the Native Americans living in Rhode Island today are Narragansetts. Long House, in Charlestown, is the Narragansetts' tribal headquarters. There they keep their heritage alive through traditional crafts, an annual powwow, and other celebrations.

Most of the new Rhode Islanders in the colonial period were English Protestants. In the 1820s, when the textile mills and metals factories were swinging into high production, great waves of job-seeking immigrants swept ashore. Most of these were Irish Catholics fleeing Ireland's severe economic conditions. Descendants of these Irish people remain the state's largest population group today.

The Civil War period brought French-Canadians to Rhode Island's factories and mills, as well as small numbers of Swedes and Germans. In Woonsocket today, French is still the first language among many of those of French-Canadian ancestry. Rhode Island's whaling ventures attracted seamen from Portugal and Portugal's Cape Verde Islands, off the west African coast. Today, many descendants of these Portuguese immigrants are concentrated in Providence's Fox Point community.

From the 1890s on, another great wave of immigration brought in thousands of southern and eastern Europeans. Poles, Lithuanians, Armenians, Ukrainians, Greeks, Syrians, Lebanese, Germans, and Russians were among those who came to Rhode Island during this time. The largest group in this wave were Italians, whose descendants make up a significant portion of the state's present population. The flavor of old Italy is still alive in Providence's Little Italy on Federal Hill, where Italian bakeries, restaurants, and espresso shops line the streets.

The decades after 1950 saw an influx of blacks, Portuguese islanders, Caribbean islanders, and Southeast Asian refugees. It is easy to see that the state of Rhode Island is, as one writer has called it, an "ethnic laboratory."

RELIGIOUS FREEDOM: THE LIVELY EXPERIMENT

When King Charles II of England granted the Rhode Island colony its royal charter in 1663, he proclaimed the colony's purpose: "To hold forth a lively experiment that a most flourishing civil state may stand and best be maintained with full liberty in religious concernments."

When Roger Williams founded the settlement of Providence in 1636, he declared that all people who lived there could worship as they pleased. Soon Williams's little colony was a refuge for Quakers, Jews, Puritans, Congregationalists, Anglicans, Catholics,

Historic buildings such as Newport's Trinity Church (left) and the Friends' Meeting House (above) reflect the state's long-standing reputation as a place of religious tolerance.

and many others as well. Though religious freedom was a shocking concept in the 1600s, this freedom would become one of the cornerstones of the new United States of America.

The overwhelming majority of Rhode Island's nineteenth-century immigrants were Roman Catholics. As a result, Rhode Island today is the most Catholic state in the country. Sixty-four percent of Rhode Islanders are members of the Roman Catholic church. The state also has substantial numbers of Jews, Episcopalians, Presbyterians, Quakers, and members of many other faiths.

POLITICS

In the 1800s and early 1900s, political tensions in Rhode Island ran high. There was a constant struggle between the Republican elite, made up of mill owners, landowners, and other wealthy aristocrats; and the Democratic working-class people, most of whom were recent immigrants.

Portuguese Catholics in Bristol celebrating the annual Santo Cristo Festival

During the American Civil War (1861-1865), Rhode Island sided with the antislavery Republican party. Republican sentiments in the state became so strong, in fact, that Rhode Islanders supported the Republican presidential candidate in nearly every election from 1856 through 1924.

Meanwhile, as Rhode Island's industrial cities swelled with laborers, the state's Democrats clamored for a stronger voice in their local and national governments. When Roman Catholic Democrat Al Smith ran for president in 1928, Rhode Island finally broke its long-standing Republican tradition. Rhode Island's voters supported Smith overwhelmingly. Although Smith lost the election, the state's ethnic, working-class majority—largely Catholic—had finally found its voice. The state's voters supported Democrats in twelve out of the sixteen presidential elections from 1928 through 1988. Voting patterns in state elections have followed roughly the same lines.

HATHAWAY HIGH
1498

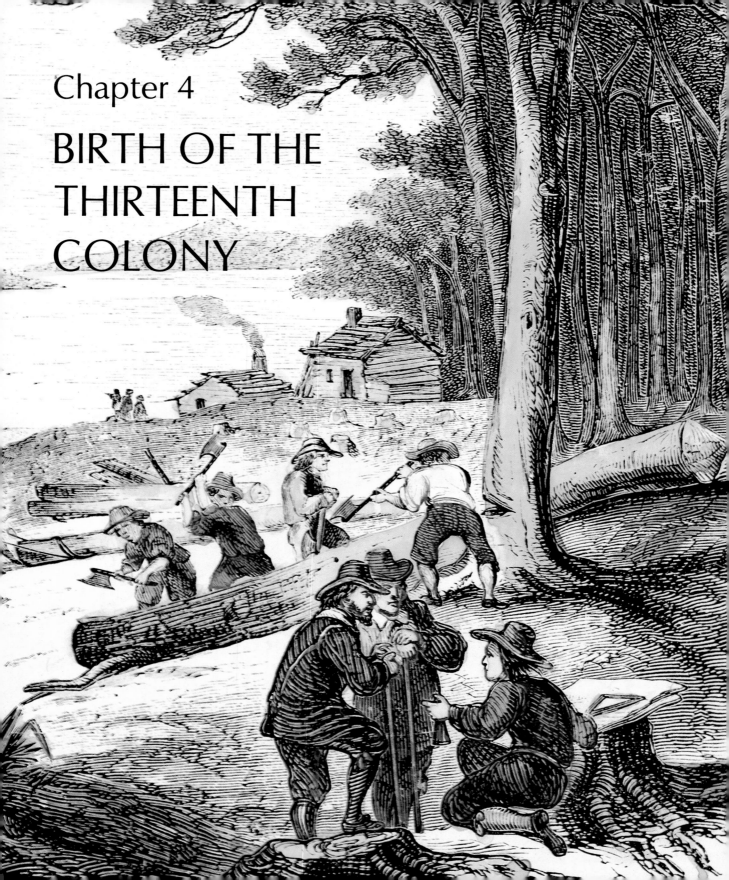

Chapter 4

BIRTH OF THE THIRTEENTH COLONY

BIRTH OF THE THIRTEENTH COLONY

THE FIRST RHODE ISLANDERS

Before white settlers arrived in Rhode Island, five groups of
Native Americans lived in the area. Along the south coast were
the Niantics. To the north and west were the Nipmucks. The
largest group was the Narragansetts, who occupied what is now
Providence and the west coast of Narragansett Bay. Across the
bay, on the eastern coast, lived the Wampanoags, enemies of the
Narragansetts. The Pequots occupied the Connecticut coastal area
around Rhode Island's southwestern tip. All five tribes belonged
to the Algonquian language group, a large family of tribes who
lived throughout the northeastern United States and were related
by language and customs.

When European settlers first arrived in Rhode Island in the
early 1600s, there were about ten thousand Native Americans in
the region. They raised corn, beans, and squash, hunted in the rich
forest lands, and caught fish and shellfish along the shores. They
lived by an impressive moral and legal code, and justice was
meted out by judges who were also spiritual leaders.

EARLY VISITORS

Although Roger Williams is honored as the father of Rhode
Island, he was not the first European to visit the area. It is possible
that Portuguese navigators visited Rhode Island in the early
1500s. Miguel Cortereal set out from Newfoundland in 1502,

A 1681 portrait
of the son of
a Niantic chief

sailing south along the Atlantic coast. He may well have reached
Rhode Island, although no one will ever know for sure. Sadly, his
ship was lost at sea.

In 1524, Italian navigator Giovanni da Verrazano, sailing for
France, explored Narragansett Bay. Although Verrazano wrote a
glowing account of the bay and its fertile islands, France took little
interest in his discoveries at the time.

In 1614, Dutch navigator Adriaen Block spotted an island in the
Atlantic Ocean just south of Rhode Island's mainland. The Indians
living there called it *Manisses*, meaning "isle of the little god."
Block charted its location on his maps and labeled it *Adriaen's
Eylandt*. Eventually it came to be called Block Island.

In the following decades, European colonists began settling in
the area. William Blackstone, an Anglican minister, moved to the
Massachusetts wilderness in the 1620s, hoping to get away from
civilization. He made his home near a spring, and when others

moved into the area, Blackstone generously shared his spring with them. The settlement grew, eventually becoming the town of Boston, Massachusetts.

Blackstone, cherishing his solitude, moved farther into the wilderness in 1635. This time he settled in what is now the town of Cumberland, Rhode Island, near the river that is now named for him. After Providence was established the following year, Blackstone would sometimes ride into the village on his cream-colored bull, handing out apples from his orchard to children.

THE PROVIDENCE SETTLEMENT

Though William Blackstone may have been Rhode Island's first white settler, he did nothing to build a colony. Actually, the area where he lived was part of Massachusetts until 1747. The person who is honored as the founder of Rhode Island is Roger Williams. In 1630, he and his wife, Mary, left England for the Massachusetts Bay Colony in the New World. A minister in the Church of England, or Anglican church, Williams had begun to disagree with the church's teachings. England's church and government at that time were united under the same leaders. This meant that any disagreement with the church was treated as a political crime. Dissidents like Roger Williams were in danger of imprisonment, torture, and even execution. A group of people called Puritans, who wished to purify the church of its corruptions, left England and founded the New World colonies of Massachusetts Bay, Plymouth, and several others.

Unfortunately, Roger Williams found that the Puritan ministers and magistrates in Massachusetts also were intolerant. Though they had left England seeking the freedom to practice their own religion, they had no tolerance for the beliefs of others. Williams soon came into conflict with the Puritan leaders for preaching that government had no right to dictate people's religious beliefs. Another of his "dangerous opinions" was that the colonists had no right to take land from the Indians.

Several times, Williams was called before the Massachusetts court and ordered to take back his teachings, but he refused. Finally, in January 1636, the governor of Massachusettts issued an order that Williams be shipped back to England. Warned that he was about to be seized, Williams slipped from his home in the middle of the night. With a handful of friends, he trekked through the frozen swamps, snowy thickets, and icy streams of the Massachusetts wilderness.

Fortunately, Williams had become friends with Wampanoag chief Ousamequin (also known as Massasoit), whose winter headquarters were in the area. On the east bank of the Seekonk River, at what is now Rumford, Rhode Island, Massasoit gave Williams and his followers food and shelter. In the spring, the refugees built houses and sowed crops. But officials of the Plymouth Colony told Williams that he was trespassing in Plymouth and must leave.

The little band of exiles paddled their canoes down the Seekonk River to a hill where the Moshassuck and Pawtuxet rivers flow together, at the head of Narragansett Bay. Finding a gushing spring on the eastern bank of the Moshassuck, they settled down. Williams purchased the land from Massasoit and two Narragansett leaders who were also close friends of his, Canonicus and Miantonomi.

The land was divided into plots, houses were built, and crops were sown. Williams named his little settlement *Providence,* saying that it was God's providence, or watchful care, that had gotten him and his followers through the wilderness.

Roger Williams was welcomed by the Wampanoags (above) when he fled to Rhode Island in 1636. Two years later, Anne Hutchinson came to Rhode Island after she, too, was banished from Massachusetts for preaching "wayward" beliefs (left).

PORTSMOUTH, NEWPORT, AND WARWICK

As word spread about Williams's new town, other people seeking religious freedom left Massachusetts for Providence. In 1638 came William Coddington, John Clarke, and followers of Anne Hutchinson, who had been tried and convicted for her "wayward" religious beliefs. Williams arranged with Canonicus and Miantonomi for the newcomers to settle on Aquidneck Island in Narragansett Bay. There they founded the settlement of Pocasset (renamed Portsmouth in 1643). Anne Hutchinson and her husband, William, soon joined them.

The Pocasset settlers, however, continued to argue about religious freedom and about separation of religion and government. Finally, Coddington and several others decided to leave and set up their own town elsewhere. In April 1639, this group moved to a harbor on the south end of the island, which they named Newport.

Meanwhile, a fiery troublemaker named Samuel Gorton was becoming embroiled in religious and political disputes with

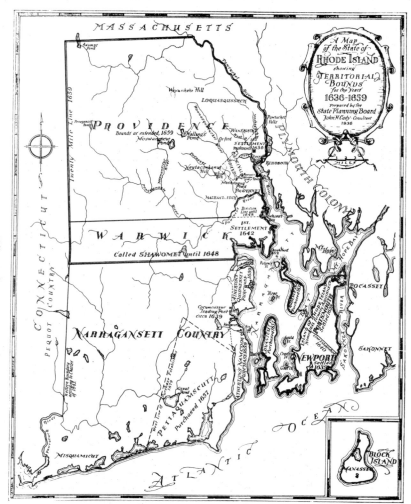

A map showing the boundaries of Rhode Island in the mid-1600s

leaders in both Portsmouth and Providence. Gorton was known throughout the colonies as the "Firebrand of New England." He and his followers eventually purchased an enormous tract of land to the south of Providence, called Shawomet, from the Narragansett Indians. Here, in 1643, the Gortonists founded the coastal settlement of Warwick.

THE COLONY IS BORN

Massachusetts officials soon made several attempts to exert control over the four new settlements. Roger Williams felt that

Providence, Warwick, and the two Aquidneck Island communities would be better able to protect themselves from outside interference if they joined together. In 1643, he journeyed to London to obtain a patent, or charter, that would officially unite the mainland and island settlements into one colony. The charter, granted in 1644, assured that religious and political freedom would prevail in "the Providence Plantations in the Narragansett Bay." In 1647, Providence, Portsmouth, Newport, and Warwick united under this charter.

Back on Aquidneck Island (renamed the Island of Rhode Island in 1644), William Coddington was working behind Williams's back. He wanted the Island of Rhode Island to join the newly formed New England Confederation or to ally with the Massachusetts or Plymouth colonies. When Williams returned from London and began organizing the new colony's government, Coddington fought his every move. In 1648, Coddington went to London and asked to be made governor of the Island of Rhode Island and nearby Conanicut Island. His request was granted in 1651.

In December 1651, accompanied by John Clarke, the untiring Williams made yet another arduous journey by sea to England. After pleading with authorities, Williams and Clarke succeeded in getting them to take back Coddington's appointment. Thus Williams kept his position as governor of the colony.

REFUGE FOR THE PERSECUTED

The colony of Rhode Island, meanwhile, was becoming known far and wide as a safe haven for those persecuted for their religious beliefs. Williams himself had spent his life seeking to follow his own conscience. Fleeing the persecutions of the Church of England, he had at first aligned himself with the Puritans of

Massachusetts Bay. Next, fleeing the Puritans, he escaped to Providence and continued preaching his own brand of religion. In 1639, he became convinced that infant baptism, which the Puritans practiced, was not sufficient for salvation. He began to believe and preach that adults should be baptized as a sign of their faith. Gathering followers of this belief, Williams founded America's first Baptist congregation. Still seeking to follow his conscience, however, he left the Baptists and became what he called a Seeker, or one who humbly seeks God's will.

All the while, Williams continued to defend the right of all people to follow their own consciences. This was good news for the members of the Society of Friends, also known as Quakers. In Massachusetts and Connecticut, Quakers had been persecuted for their pacifism and for their refusal to take an oath of allegiance to either the king of England or the Puritan church. In the late 1650s, harsh laws were enacted against Quakers in Massachusetts and Connecticut, forcing them to seek homes elsewhere. In 1657, a group of Quakers arrived in Newport. Members of this group established the nation's first Quaker meetinghouse there in 1699.

In 1658, attracted by the promise of religious freedom, a group of Spanish and Portuguese Jewish families from the Caribbean Islands arrived in Newport and formed a congregation. Newport's Touro Synagogue, dedicated in 1763, is today North America's oldest Jewish synagogue. In 1686, forty-five French Protestant (Huguenot) families, fleeing persecution in France, settled in the town of East Greenwich.

THE SECOND CHARTER

In the 1660s, because of political upheavals in England, Rhode Island's status was again in question. England's parliament had

Touro Synagogue in Newport, built in 1763, is America's oldest Jewish synagogue.

been ruling England since the overthrow of King Charles I in 1649. In 1660, the monarchy was restored when a new king, Charles II, took the throne. Rhode Islanders did not know whether their charter remained in effect under the new king.

John Clarke, still in England since his 1651 trip, succeeded in obtaining a new charter from Charles II in 1663. This "Charter of Rhode Island and Providence Plantations" gave Rhode Island the lengthy official name it still carries today. It also clarified the colony's boundaries once and for all.

The new charter spelled out the colony's philosophy quite clearly: Rhode Island was to be a "lively experiment" in freedom of religion. It was also given broad rights of self-government. This was unheard-of for a New World colony. Previous colonies had been appointed royal governors, who ruled in the name of England. Rhode Island, however, would be free to elect its own governor and government officials. Thus Rhode Island also became a "lively experiment" in democracy—and the first true democracy in the New World.

INDIAN AFFAIRS

The issue of Indians' rights had been a serious area of dispute between Roger Williams and the Massachusetts authorities. While in Massachusetts, Williams had spent time getting to know the Indians of the area. He learned their customs, studied their language, and came to respect them deeply. He eventually published a book on Indian language entitled *A Key into the Language of America*. Williams believed that Indians had the right to their own religion. He also believed that their land was their own and that colonists should be allowed to take it only by a legal transfer of property rights.

Williams worked hard to maintain friendly relations with Rhode Island's native people. He also helped make peace between the Narragansetts and the Wampanoags. He procured land for his settlements through fair negotiations with the Narragansett chiefs. Most other colonists obtained Indian land simply by moving in and taking it over. As a result, conflicts broke out frequently between colonists and Indians.

KING PHILIP'S WAR

Pushed to their limit by the 1670s, the Narragansetts, Wampanoags, and others joined forces. They planned to retaliate against white settlers in New England who had taken so much of their ancestral lands. They united under Wampanoag chief Metacomet, whom the colonists called King Philip. In 1675, King

In 1675, Wampanoag Chief Metacomet, whom the American colonists called King Philip, organized several Indian tribes for a concerted assault against the white settlers.

Philip's followers began attacking colonists throughout New England. Troops from Massachusetts, Plymouth, and Connecticut fought back on all fronts without mercy.

This conflict was known as King Philip's War. It had its climax in the Great Swamp Fight near Kingston, Rhode Island, on December 19, 1675. In this swamp, the Narragansetts and Wampanoags, with their wives and children, were camping for the winter. While a furious blizzard raged, the colonists attacked the camp, burned fortifications and homes, and killed all who tried to escape. King Philip, who was not in the camp, was killed a few months later. Within another two years, colonists throughout New England had succeeded in breaking the Indians' power once and for all.

Roger Williams, champion of Indians' rights, was saddened to see the downfall of his old friends. He continued to live in Providence, managing the colony's affairs, until his death in 1683 at around the age of eighty.

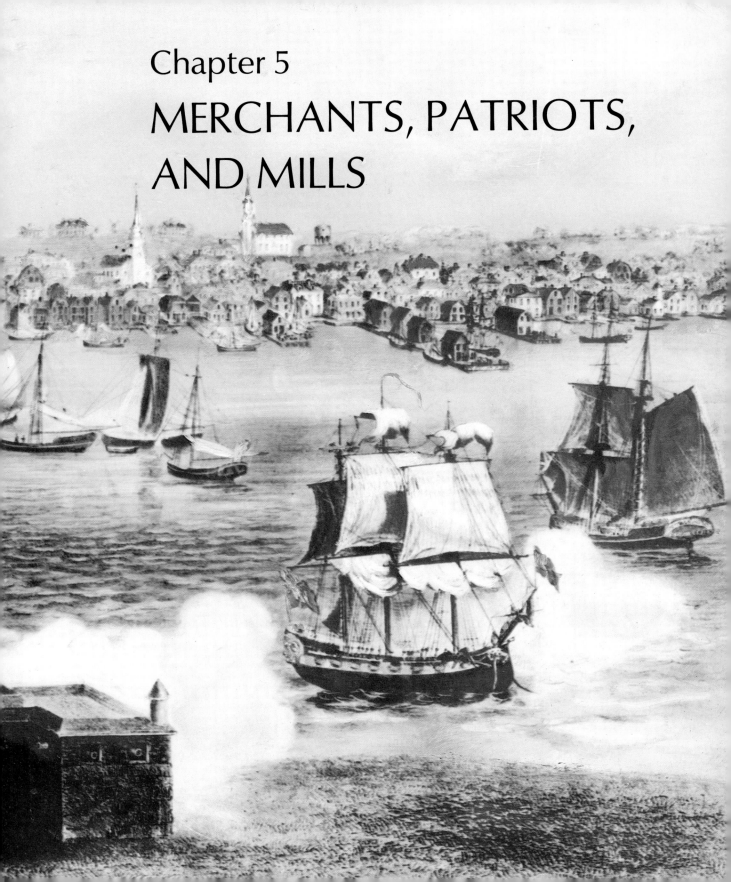

Chapter 5
MERCHANTS, PATRIOTS, AND MILLS

MERCHANTS, PATRIOTS, AND MILLS

Through the late 1600s and early 1700s, agriculture was the mainstay of Rhode Island's economy. The fertile bay islands, coastal areas, and southern lowlands produced an abundance of corn, beans, flax, livestock, and dairy products. From the north and west came apples and timber. The Narragansett Pacer, a prized breed of horse, was developed and sold throughout New England. Aristocratic farmers known as the Narragansett Planters ran plantations as lavish as those in the South. Slaves worked as field hands and as servants in the planters' elegant homes.

THE RISE OF SHIPPING

With its surplus of farm products and its fine natural harbors, Rhode Island soon turned to exporting. Newport became the colony's shipping capital, with the port of Providence bustling as well. Wealthy merchants' fleets plied the seas as far as Africa, the Mediterranean Sea, the Red Sea, and the Pacific Ocean.

Sailing on a merchant ship was quite an adventure, and young men swarmed the harbor towns to sign on as seamen. Though most voyages were successful, many ships were lost to pirates or stormy seas. Lost ships were reported to Newport's notary public, who assigned official blame. Even if the weather was the culprit, it had to stand accused. On the loss of the sloop *Endeavour* in 1723, the notary concluded: "Wherefore I . . . do hereby Publickly and Solemnly Protest against the said Boisterous Winds and Seas as the only Occasion of all the Losses aforesaid. . . ."

CORDIALS,
Warranted pure
MADE and SOLD BY
John Slocum
IN
Newport R. Island.

TO BE SOLD, by
JOHN LYON,
At REHOBOTH:
TWENTY-THREE fine healthy young Slaves, just arrived from the Coast of Africa. —For Directions and further Information, apply to WILLIAM PROUD, in Providence.

Rhode Island merchants involved in the triangle trade used trade cards (left) and newspaper notices (above) to advertise the sale of slaves and liquor products made from sugar or molasses.

THE TRIANGLE TRADE

It did not take Newport's merchants long to discover a business more profitable than exporting: the triangle trade. Ships on the triangle trade route sailed a three-point course that included Newport, Africa, and the West Indies. Their cargoes were molasses, rum, and slaves. First, molasses was shipped from West Indies sugar plantations to Newport. At some thirty distilleries around the colony, the molasses was transformed into rum.

Merchants then shipped the rum to Africa to trade it for slaves. A healthy black male, for instance, might cost one hundred gallons of rum. The slaves were literally packed below the decks, where many died during their voyage. On some voyages, more than half the slaves died from disease or starvation. Still, the profits from selling the surviving slaves were so great that the trade continued. Laden with human cargo, the ships headed back to Newport or to the West Indies, where the slaves were sold at a hefty profit. The profits bought more molasses, and the cycle began again.

The triangle trade merchants were not beyond cheating each other. One Newport shipper, whose brother was sending him molasses from the West Indies, had constant complaints. After an especially bad shipment, he wrote to his brother that it was "hard to say whether it be molasses or water."

THE BROWN FAMILY

In Providence, the Brown brothers—Nicholas, Joseph, John, and Moses—emerged as the leading merchant family. Together they transformed Providence into one of New England's major shipping centers. Aggressive dealers in the triangle trade, the Browns bought and sold slaves and distilled rum. They also pioneered the manufacture of spermaceti candles (made from a whale by-product) and opened up the colonies' trade with China.

Though a strong opponent of slavery himself, Moses Brown benefited from the family fortunes along with his brothers. Moses's textile mill, north of Providence, was the first in America to become mechanized using waterpower. Rhode Island College was renamed Brown University after Nicholas Brown made a huge donation to the school. John Brown used part of his fortune to build a magnificent, fourteen-room house in Providence. The house was designed by his architect brother Joseph. Joseph also designed Providence's First Baptist Meeting House.

BRITISH RESTRICTIONS

From the mid-1600s through the mid-1700s, England fought one war after another with its rivals in the colonies or on the seas. In British wars with the Dutch, the Spanish, and the French, Rhode Island contributed its money, men, and ships. When a war

In 1770, after Nicholas Brown donated extensive funds and lands to Rhode Island College, the school moved from Warren to Providence, where it was renamed Brown University (above).

was on, some private ship captains were hired by the government as privateers—they were to capture enemy ships at sea and disable them. Naturally, this included looting their cargoes, too. There came to be a fine line, if any at all, between a pirate and a privateer. Both piracy and smuggling were becoming profitable industries in Rhode Island.

To turn more of the profits their way, British officials moved to clamp down on shipping—both legal and illegal—in the colonies. They imposed restrictions and high taxes not only on imports from other countries but also on manufacturing in the colonies. This would force the colonists to rely on goods manufactured and shipped by the British. In 1699, the colonies were forbidden to manufacture woolen goods. The manufacture of hats was outlawed in 1732, and iron in 1751.

With the Molasses Act of 1733, England attempted to control the foreign molasses trade by imposing high import taxes, or

Angered by England's attempts to police Narragansett Bay, a group of Rhode Islanders set fire to the British schooner *Gaspee* on June 9, 1772.

duties. The British wanted the colonies to buy only the sugar and molasses that came from the British West Indies. That source, however, could not provide enough of these products to meet the colonists' needs. Most Rhode Island shippers found illegal ways— smuggling, in particular—to keep from paying the duties. In 1763, British patrol ships began cruising Rhode Island's harbors and seizing ships suspected of smuggling molasses.

The Sugar Act of 1764 further restricted the importation of foreign sugar and molasses and added taxes on tea, lead, and other necessities. It was the Stamp Act of 1765, however, that most outraged the colonists. This measure levied taxes on newspapers, legal documents, playing cards, and other paper items. Throughout the colonies, protesters calling themselves the Sons of Liberty burned tax announcements and hung and burned stuffed effigies (dummies) that represented the tax collectors.

Rhode Islanders were outraged over these harsh impositions. For more than a century, they had been accustomed to governing their own affairs. With more freedom to lose from the British restrictions, they reacted more violently than other colonists.

RHODE ISLANDERS FIGHT BACK

On July 9, 1764, Newporters shot a cannon at the British patrol ship *St. John* and tore a hole in its mainsail. On June 4, 1765, a crowd of Newporters burned a boat from the British navy recruiting ship *Maidstone*. Another patrol ship, the *Liberty*, was scuttled and torched at Newport in 1769. British officials tried their best to investigate the attacks, but to no avail. From the governor on down to the waterfront derelicts, Rhode Islanders protected each other with elaborate lies.

The most notorious attack occurred on the night of June 9, 1772. While chasing a suspected smuggler, the British schooner *Gaspee* ran aground on Namquit Point (now Gaspee Point). Providence merchant John Brown organized an attack party that shot and wounded the *Gaspee's* captain and burned the ship to its water line. A team of British investigators was unable to turn up a shred of evidence against the perpetrators.

Rhode Island's blatant defiance of the British gave the other colonists courage. Enraged by the Tea Act of 1773, Bostonians dumped a valuable shipment of British tea into Boston Harbor. To punish the colonists for the Boston Tea Party, as the incident was called, England passed severe measures that became known in America as the Intolerable Acts. England also closed the port of Boston and sent troops to occupy the city. The Rhode Island General Assembly soon suggested that the colonies band together for mutual support. In 1774, the thirteen American colonies convened the First Continental Congress in Philadelphia, Pennsylvania. Rhode Island was the first colony to elect delegates to the congress, choosing Samuel Ward and Stephen Hopkins, who had been Rhode Island's governor for many years.

Tensions continued to rise as clashes arose between colonists and British troops. Finally, on April 18, 1775, gunfire broke out between the two in Concord, Massachusetts. The American Revolution had begun.

REVOLUTION!

Now, fighting for their own independence instead of for British foreign wars, Rhode Islanders were eager to offer their money, ships, and men. The Continental Congress named Rhode Islander Esek Hopkins, a former privateer and the brother of Stephen Hopkins, as commander-in-chief of the Continental navy. General George Washington, commander-in-chief of the Continental army, picked Rhode Islander Nathanael Greene as his second-in-command. Greene served heroically in the siege of Boston, the Battle of Long Island, and the Battle of Monmouth. Washington eventually put him in command of the Continental army's forces in the South.

On May 4, 1776, Rhode Island officially renounced its allegiance to England's King George III. This was the first declaration of independence in the colonies. Two months later, on July 4, 1776, the thirteen colonies as a whole issued their Declaration of Independence. Signing the declaration on behalf of Rhode Island was Stephen Hopkins.

The revolution took a heavy toll on Rhode Island's economy. British troops occupied Newport in 1776 and virtually demolished the town. Shipping came to a halt, and the British burned

A modern painting depicting Rhode Island's Black Regiment fighting in the 1778 Battle of Rhode Island

whatever they could—including hundreds of houses—for firewood. Much of Newport's population simply left town.

France, England's longtime enemy, sent troops to aid the colonists in their struggle. In the 1778 Battle of Rhode Island, French and American soldiers battled the British in Newport and Portsmouth. Thanks to Rhode Island's Black Regiment, made up of former slaves, the colonists held firm against the British, though they failed to drive them out. When the British finally left Newport in 1779, it was said that they had "nothing left to destroy."

In July 1780, six thousand French forces under Count Rochambeau arrived in Newport and made it their base of operation. The entire Continental army welcomed these valiant French troops. They were a major factor in the American victory

Count Rochambeau, who landed in Newport in 1780 with French troops (right) to aid the Americans in the Revolutionary War, is honored in Newport with a statue (above).

at the Battle of Yorktown in 1781, which virtually crippled the British cause.

CONSTITUTIONAL STRUGGLES

After the Treaty of Paris ended the war in 1783, the new United States set about enacting a constitution. By 1790, twelve of the thirteen states had ratified, or approved, the United States Constitution. Only Rhode Island held out. Many Rhode Islanders were afraid of losing their cherished independence to a federal authority. Others, in the Rhode Island tradition of civil liberties, refused to approve the Constitution unless it included a bill of rights or abolished slavery.

Though the slave trade had been important to Rhode Island's economy, Rhode Islanders with antislavery sentiments, including

Newport as it appeared just after the Revolutionary War

Moses Brown, fought to end slavery. In 1774, Rhode Island
became the first colony to prohibit the importation of slaves. A
law providing for the gradual freeing of slaves was passed in 1784.
In 1787, the slave trade in Rhode Island was finally outlawed.
Despite the abolitionists' efforts, however, the law was poorly
enforced. Moses Brown even took his brother John to court for
engaging in the slave trade, though the jury did not convict him.

   The other twelve states grew impatient with Rhode Island's
reluctance to ratify the Constitution. Some even suggested leaving
Rhode Island out of the Union or merging it into Massachusetts or
Connecticut. Finally, assured that a bill of rights would be added,
the state's constitutional convention ratified the Constitution on
May 29, 1790, by a 34-32 vote.

The spinning room of an 1830s New England textile mill

PAWTUCKET'S INDUSTRIAL REVOLUTION

Meanwhile, Rhode Islanders busied themselves with business pursuits to recover from the devastating effects of the revolution. Their economic well-being had long been crippled by England's harsh manufacturing and trade restrictions. Now that they were no longer under England's reign, the door was open for them to become producers themselves. Little did they realize that they were fostering yet another American revolution—this time, an industrial one.

Providence merchant Moses Brown operated a cotton-spinning mill in Pawtucket. In 1790, he hired Samuel Slater, a British textile worker. In England, Slater had worked with waterpowered spinning machines called Arkwright machines. The Arkwright process was a closely guarded secret. Anyone who worked in a British textile mill was forbidden to leave the country.

Disguised as a farmer, however, Slater had sneaked out of England. At Moses Brown's Pawtucket mill, he reconstructed the

Slater Mill Historic Site in Pawtucket preserves the nation's first water-driven cotton mill.

Arkwright process entirely from memory. Turned round and round by the waters of the Blackstone River, a huge waterwheel powered the mill's machinery through a series of interlocking gears. In 1793, Slater left Brown and opened his own mill. Soon, other waterpowered factories sprang up along the Blackstone. David Wilkinson opened a mill in 1810 that manufactured metal tools and equipment. By the early 1800s, Pawtucket was a boomtown.

This marked a revolution in American manufacturing—and in the American way of life. Now that the making of goods was machine-based, production no longer had to depend on the time of day, the seasons of the year, or human fatigue. As long as water flowed, the machines could run twenty-four hours a day, every day of the year. And since there were always plenty of hungry people who needed jobs, there were always enough workers to tend the machines.

Chapter 6

AN INDUSTRIAL
POWER

AN INDUSTRIAL POWER

IMMIGRANT LABOR

The face of Rhode Island changed as waves of immigrants
poured in to work at the mills. Irish Catholics made up the first
wave, arriving in the 1820s and continuing to immigrate through
the 1800s. Later groups included French-Canadians, Swedes,
Germans, Portuguese, and southern and eastern Europeans.

Whole families went to work in the mills, including children. In
some plants, *most* of the employees were children. Their smaller
hands and bodies were found to be very useful. Children could
reach between rows of whirling bobbins to catch loose threads or
crawl under moving machinery to pick up dropped parts.
Industrial illnesses, injuries, and even deaths were not uncommon
among the factory workers. They inhaled dust and fibers, slipped
on wet floors, and caught body parts in the machines. As early as
1824, women textile workers in Pawtucket went on strike to get
better working conditions. Soon, other workers began forming
labor unions, sometimes battling bitterly against management to
improve wages, hours, and safety standards.

THE DORR REBELLION

Between 1800 and 1850, Rhode Island's population more than
doubled, growing from 69,122 to 147,545. In the 1840s alone, the
population swelled nearly 36 percent. Yet in 1840, only about

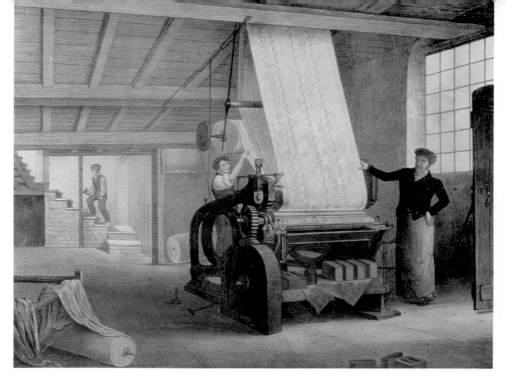

In the 1800s, Rhode Island textile mills used machines such as this to print patterns onto finished cloth.

40 percent of Rhode Island's adult white males could vote. Rhode Island's 1663 charter gave voting rights only to landholders, and the growing working-class population did not own land. Instead, most of them lived in crowded tenement housing in factory towns.

People grew more and more discontent with the unfair voting requirements and unequal representation. Even though cities had the largest populations, rural areas had the greatest representation in the state legislature. A reform movement sprang up, with Providence attorney Thomas Dorr taking the lead. Calling themselves the "People's party," Dorr and his followers held their own "People's Convention" in 1841. The convention ratified a new state constitution that extended voting rights to all adult males. The People's party then held their own statewide election in which Dorr was elected governor. These actions became known as the Dorr Rebellion.

A statue of Ambrose Burnside graces Kennedy Plaza in downtown Providence.

The state's regular government, meanwhile, refused to recognize Dorr's authority and used armed force against his followers. For his part in the rebellion, Dorr was tried for treason and jailed. The effort, however, was a success. It forced the state legislators to change voting requirements, redivide legislative districts more fairly, and enact a new state constitution. This constitution of 1843 is still in effect today, though it has been modernized and amended over the years.

In the second half of the nineteenth century, political sentiments in Rhode Island settled into a clear pattern. On the majority side were the Republicans, most of whom were Protestants. In the minority, but gaining ground, were the Democrats, most of whom were Irish Catholics.

On the eve of the American Civil War (1861-1865), Rhode Islanders were reluctant to fight against the slaveholding South. After all, Rhode Island's textile industry depended on southern cotton produced by slave labor. Nevertheless, twenty-four thousand of the state's men volunteered for the Union army. Rhode Islander Ambrose Burnside was chosen to command the Army of the Potomac during the war. He later served Rhode Island as governor and as a United States senator. Burnside's bushy whiskers became fashionable and were named "sideburns" after him.

ECONOMIC GROWTH—AND DECLINE

Rhode Island's economy, and its population, continued to grow throughout the 1800s. Italians were the largest new ethnic group to arrive after 1890. Others came from Poland, Russia, Germany, Greece, Armenia, Lithuania, and the Ukraine. Between 1850 and 1910, the state's population nearly quadrupled. The textile mills were exporting thread, yarn, and fabrics to destinations all over the world. The jewelry and silverware industries were flourishing as well. In the 1880s, the United States Navy, born in Newport during the American Revolution, opened a naval base and the Navy War College in Newport.

In the late 1800s, Newport became a popular summer vacation spot for the wealthy industrialists of the East Coast. Such families as the Vanderbilts, Astors, and Morgans built splendid summer homes along Newport's oceanfront, where they lived and entertained in lavish style.

Many of Rhode Island's factories were busy making military supplies during World War I (1914-1918). Combat ships, cargo ships, chemicals, and munitions rolled off the state's assembly lines and into service areas. Unfortunately, though the end of the war was welcomed, it meant unemployment for large numbers of factory workers. But that was only the beginning of an even larger economic decline. To find cheaper labor and cut down on shipping costs, Rhode Island's textile mills began moving to the South in the 1920s. This created serious labor problems and left hundreds more workers unemployed. Rhode Island's labor-union movement stepped up its activities. In the 1930s, the effects of the nation's great economic depression put still more workers out on the streets.

THE BLOODLESS REVOLUTION

The Democratic party continued to gain strength in Rhode Island in the early decades of the 1900s. Ethnic groups and laborers hoped to oust the Republicans, who held the reins of power in the state legislature and the governor's office. When Al Smith, a Roman Catholic, became the nation's Democratic presidential candidate in 1928, Rhode Island's Democrats began to feel that their time had come.

Democrat Theodore Francis Green, elected governor in 1933, finally turned state politics around. First, he and his colleagues helped Democrats win a majority of the seats in the state senate. Then, on New Year's Day of 1935—and, as legend has it, in a fifteen-minute swoop—Green cleared the Republicans out of the state's executive offices and set up the state government afresh. Ever since this "Bloodless Revolution," as it was called, labor-oriented Democrats have been the state's ruling party. Since 1930, Rhode Island voters have sent only one Republican to the United States Senate.

WORLD WAR II

World War II, which began in 1939, brought an upswing in Rhode Island's economy. Wartime industries in the state put

President Franklin Roosevelt visiting the Naval Torpedo Station on
Goat Island, which produced thousands of torpedoes during World War II

thousands of people to work. At the Naval Torpedo Station on
Newport's Goat Island, workers—mostly women—produced
seventeen thousand torpedoes between 1941 and 1945. The
Quonset Point Naval Air Station near Davisville developed the
famous Quonset huts. These portable, prefabricated sheet-metal
structures were used for barracks, hospitals, warehouses, and
many other purposes during the war.

When World War II ended in 1945, the state was once again
plagued by unemployment. More jobs were lost as more textile
operations moved to the South. By 1949, the state's
unemployment rate had climbed to 17 percent.

ECONOMIC TURNAROUND

In the 1950s, Rhode Island began to develop new sectors of its
economy. Although the state continued to manufacture textiles, it

no longer depended on them. Soon, much of Rhode Island's labor force was going to work in plants producing electronics equipment, chemicals, machinery, and plastics. By the close of the 1960s, only 3 percent of Rhode Islanders were unemployed.

Rhode Island's General Assembly faced another upheaval in the 1960s. The traditional political dominance of Rhode Island's Yankee landowners had greatly influenced the organization of state government. Before 1966, the boundaries of the state's legislative districts were so unevenly drawn that many small, rural towns had a greater voice in the state legislature than urban areas with much larger populations. A small town of two hundred people might be represented by one state senator, while Providence—the state's most populous city—also had only one senator. After the United States Supreme Court issued its "one man—one vote" ruling in 1964, Rhode Island reapportioned, or redrew, its legislative districts to provide the populated cities with fairer representation.

Rhode Island's population dropped slightly in the 1970s, but growing industries in the state have reversed that trend. With more than eight hundred companies engaged in making jewelry and refining precious metals, Rhode Island remains the foremost costume-jewelry manufacturer in the country. Electronics and metals industries employ one-third of all the state's manufacturing workers.

Shipbuilding continues to be an important industry in Rhode Island, just as it was in the seventeenth century. In 1974, General Dynamics Corporation opened a facility in North Kingstown for the production of nuclear-powered submarines. The United States Navy still maintains a number of installations in Rhode Island.

Several national corporations have their headquarters in the state as well. One of the largest is the conglomerate Textron. Some

The manufacture of costume jewelry became a key industry in Rhode Island in the twentieth century.

of the state's other corporations are Raytheon, maker of oceanographic equipment; Davol, which produces health-care items; Hasbro, the world's largest toy maker; and Brown and Sharpe, manufacturer of precision instruments.

An attractive resort for two centuries, Rhode Island in the 1970s and 1980s became increasingly popular with tourists. With the completion of the Newport Bridge in 1969, the boating and vacationing destination of Newport became more accessible to visitors. That same year saw the completion of Interstate 95 through Rhode Island, providing easy access to the state from Massachusetts and Connecticut. Tourism is expected to rise throughout the 1990s, as visitors from around the country—and around the world—discover the history and the natural beauty of the Ocean State.

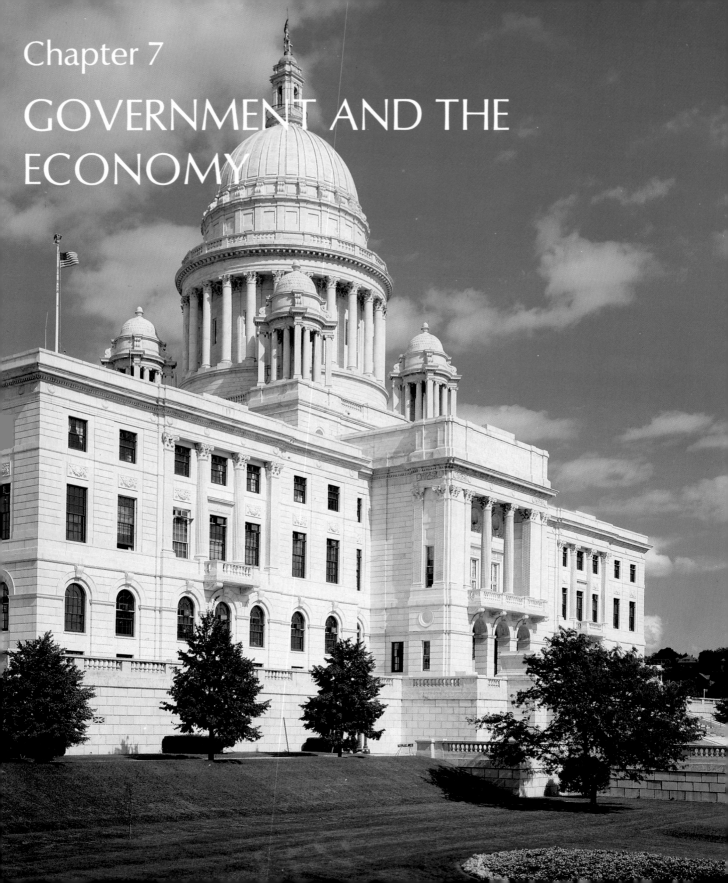

Chapter 7

GOVERNMENT AND THE ECONOMY

GOVERNMENT AND THE ECONOMY

STATE GOVERNMENT

Like the federal government, Rhode Island's state government is organized into three branches. The legislative branch makes the state's laws, the judicial branch interprets and applies them, and the executive branch enforces them. The state legislature, or General Assembly, follows the bicameral (two-house) pattern of the United States Congress. Voters elect fifty members to Rhode Island's senate and one hundred members to its house of representatives. Each member of the General Assembly is elected from a special senate or house district and serves a two-year term.

The General Assembly enjoys many governmental privileges. By a three-fifths vote, state legislators can override a governor's veto. Legislators also appoint justices to the state supreme court and establish all lower courts. Regular sessions of the General Assembly begin on the first Tuesday of every January and last for at least sixty working days. Sometimes regular sessions last longer, and special sessions may be called.

The executive branch of Rhode Island's state government owes its organization to the Bloodless Revolution of 1935. Since then, the executive branch has consisted of the governor, lieutenant governor, attorney general, secretary of state, and general treasurer. The governor, who may be elected to an unlimited number of two-year terms, appoints the heads of twenty government departments with the approval of the state senate.

Rhode Island's state supreme court is the head of its judicial branch. Its chief justice and four associate justices serve for life once the General Assembly elects them. The state supreme court has authority over all the lower courts that the General Assembly has established. It is also the highest state court to which lower-court cases may be appealed. Justices of the district courts, superior courts, and family courts are also appointed for life by the governor with the approval of the General Assembly.

The present state constitution is only the second governing document that Rhode Island has had in its entire history. Adopted in 1843 in the aftermath of the Dorr Rebellion, it has been amended (changed) more than forty times. The constitution can be amended by a majority vote of the General Assembly, followed by a majority vote of the people. In 1968, voters rejected a proposal for a new state constitution. A constitutional convention in 1988, while not producing a new constitution, resulted in many important amendments to the 1843 constitution.

LOCAL GOVERNMENT

Although Rhode Island has five counties—Providence, Kent, Washington, Bristol, and Newport—it has no county government. Instead, the state is divided into thirty-nine "municipalities," each with its own form of local government.

In Rhode Island, a municipality is actually a cross between a county and a city or town. Municipalities, much like townships elsewhere, include the rural areas surrounding a town. Thus, there are no unincorporated areas in the state; the border of each municipality touches the next. A landmark said to be "in Westerly" could be anywhere within that municipality—and far from the village of Westerly itself.

The town meeting, an old New England tradition of democracy in action, is a common form of local government in rural Rhode Island. Here townspeople meet to discuss and vote on important local issues. Some larger cities and towns have mayor-council, council-manager, or council-president forms of government. Fifteen of the thirty-nine municipalities are governed by home rule. This means that their charters, or bodies of local laws, do not have to be approved by the General Assembly.

REVENUE AND EXPENDITURES

Rhode Island's state government derives nearly half of its revenue, or income, from state taxes. Personal income taxes provide the bulk of the tax revenue, followed by Rhode Island's state sales tax. Corporation taxes, gasoline taxes, and vehicle registration fees bring in income as well. Federal grants are the state's other major source of revenue. Rhode Island then spends more than 70 percent of its government income on social services, education, health care, and public transportation.

On the local level, cities and towns build up their treasuries by collecting a property tax from their residents. Each municipality is responsible for its own public schools. It is no surprise, then, that most of the local revenue is spent on education.

EDUCATION

Early Rhode Island colonists preferred to educate their children in private schools run by their own religious groups. Even so, in 1640, Robert Lenthal's desire to "keep a public school for learning of the youth" in Newport led to the founding of one of the first public schools in the American colonies.

Brown University, in Providence, is the seventh-oldest college in the United States.

In 1800, the state imposed America's first tax for free public schools. Repealed in 1803, the tax was reinstated in 1828. Henry Barnard, who became Rhode Island's first state commissioner of education in 1845, greatly reformed the public school system. That same year saw the formation of a statewide parochial school system.

Today the governor appoints members to the state board of regents for education. The regents appoint the commissioner of education, make policies, and set standards for education in the state. Rhode Island children between the ages of seven and fifteen are required to attend school.

The state of Rhode Island maintains three public colleges. These are the University of Rhode Island, which was founded in 1892

The Rhode Island School of Design, in Providence, is one of the finest art schools in the nation.

and has its main campus in Kingston; Rhode Island College in Providence, which was founded in 1854 and is the second-oldest college in the state; and the Community College of Rhode Island, a two-year college with campuses in Warwick and Lincoln. The University of Rhode Island's oceanographic research facilities are among the finest in the country.

Most of the state's colleges are privately supported. Brown University in Providence, founded as Rhode Island College in 1764, is the state's oldest and most prestigious institution of higher learning. A member of the "Ivy League," it is the third-oldest college in New England and the seventh-oldest in the country.

Providence College is affiliated with the Dominican religious order. The Rhode Island School of Design, also in Providence, is considered by many to be the nation's finest school of fine arts and architecture. Newport's Naval War College is known as the "campus of the Navy." Johnson and Wales University in Providence prepares students for careers in the hotel and restaurant industries.

Other Rhode Island colleges include Salve Regina College, in Newport; Bryant College, in Smithfield; Roger Williams College, in Bristol; Hall Institute of Technology, in Providence; and the New England Institute of Technology, in Providence and Warwick.

ECONOMY

Beginning in the early 1800s, manufacturing grew to dominate Rhode Island's economic life. Though the state's manufacturing activities took a sharp plunge in the 1920s, manufacturing remains Rhode Island's single largest source of income. Today, about 27 percent of Rhode Island's gross state product (the total worth of all goods and services produced in the state in a year) comes from manufacturing. Twenty-eight percent of Rhode Island's labor force works in manufacturing industries.

The state's two most important manufacturing activities, jewelry and silverware production, trace their origins to Nehemiah Dodge. A Providence goldsmith and silversmith, Dodge opened his own jewelry-making business in 1794. The success of his enterprise caught on, and today the Providence area leads the country in the manufacture of costume jewelry. In 1813, one of Dodge's apprentices, Jabez Gorham, began manufacturing silver spoons on his own. Today, Gorham is the world's leading producer of sterling silver.

Next in importance among Rhode Island's manufactured goods are valves, screws, metal pipe fittings, nails, hand tools, and other fabricated metal products. Electrical equipment ranks next, with broadcasting equipment as the most important. Textiles, electronics equipment, scientific instruments, refined metals, chemicals, and plastics are some of the state's other manufactured goods.

Rhode Island is one of the nation's leading producers of silverware.

Workers in Rhode Island's service industries produce 68 percent of the state's gross state product. A little over one-fourth of these people are engaged in community or social-service industries such as schools, hospitals, hotels, advertising, and repairs. Another one-fourth work in wholesale or retail trade. With its international port facilities, Providence is an important wholesale trade center. Restaurants and stores are Rhode Island's major retail businesses, with Providence and Warwick being the major retailing centers.

MILITARY INSTALLATIONS

Rhode Island and the United States Navy have been closely associated since the navy's birth in 1775. That was the year Esek Hopkins of Providence was named the first commander-in-chief of the Continental navy.

The Arcade, in Providence, is the oldest enclosed shopping mall in the United States.

In 1941, just before the United States entered World War II, the navy expanded its Newport Naval Base. It also established a large-scale naval air station at Quonset Point. The war's famous Quonset huts were designed here. The Naval Construction Battalion Center in Davisville trained the war's "Seabees" (actually, "CBs"—members of a construction battalion). These and other facilities boosted the state's economy by employing large numbers of residents. Many other Rhode Islanders worked in munitions manufacturing facilities on Goat Island during the war.

Peace in 1945 meant unemployment for many Rhode Islanders who had worked in wartime industries. When Quonset Point was closed in 1973, more jobs were lost. However, the navy still maintains its Naval Education and Training Center, Naval Underwater System Center, and Naval War College in Newport.

The United States Navy is the largest single employer in Newport County.

In fact, the navy is the largest single employer in Newport County and, after the state's government, the largest employer in the state.

AGRICULTURE

Farmland and pastureland cover about 11 percent of Rhode Island's total land area. Along the Narragansett Bay, the firm soil known as Miami stony loam makes this the state's best farming region. The sandy Glocester stony loam of the north and west, however, is difficult to farm. Farming occupies 1 percent of the state's labor force and also brings in 1 percent of the gross state product. Nursery and greenhouse products are the leading agricultural items. Accounting for about two-thirds of the state's total agricultural income, these include ornamental shrubs, Christmas trees, and turf, or seeded soil.

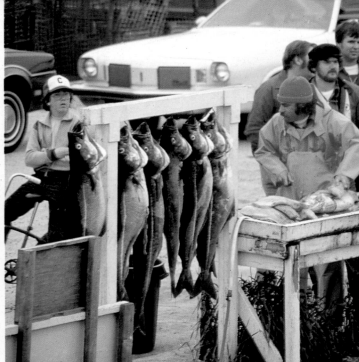

Agriculture and commercial fishing are important aspects of the state's economy.

Producing Rhode Island's second-most-important agricultural products, dairy farms around the state yield milk and other dairy foods. Potatoes are the state's most important crop, followed by hay. Sweet corn, tomatoes, snap beans, squash, and cabbage thrive in the fertile lowland soils. From Rhode Island's orchards come apples, peaches, and pears. Roadside signs throughout the rural farmlands reveal the growing practice of "pick-your-own" produce.

Chickens, eggs, and turkeys are some of Rhode Island's other farm products. The Rhode Island Red chicken, the state bird, is a breed developed in Little Compton.

Though it now accounts for only 1 percent of the state's total agricultural income, wine making has recently entered Rhode Island's agricultural economy. Row upon row of well-tended grapevines stretch through the commercial vineyards of Little Compton, Prudence Island, South Kingstown, and Cumberland.

The Port of Providence is one of the finest deep-water ports on the eastern seaboard.

MINERAL RESOURCES

Because of glacier movements during the great Ice Age, Rhode Island's soils are rocky. The state has a great variety of minerals, many of which were once important commercially. These include coal, graphite, quartzite, and bog iron. Now granite, sand, and gravel, used as construction materials, are the state's most important minerals. The hard and fine-grained Westerly granite, mined in the southwest near Westerly, is highly valued as a building stone. Crushed sandstone and limestone are also important as construction materials.

TRANSPORTATION

Though the ports of Newport and Providence flourished in colonial days, the rise of railroad transportation in the mid-1800s

Newport Bridge over Narragansett Bay

brought about their decline. Today, however, the modern Port of Providence is a bustling commercial shipping center. Located at the top of Narragansett Bay, it is one of the finest deep-water ports on the eastern seaboard. Into the Port of Providence come much of southern New England's petroleum products, as well as automobiles, lumber, chemicals, and cement. Scrap iron and manufactured goods are some of Providence's shipbound exports.

Rhode Island's major airport, Theodore Francis Green State Airport in Warwick, is also southern New England's most important commercial airfield. The approach-light system on

Green's all-weather runway enables planes to land when visibility is very low. Smaller airports are located in Smithfield, Newport, Westerly, Block Island, and North Kingstown.

Travelers driving through Rhode Island enjoy its excellent system of state and interstate highways. Most of the state's 6,300 miles (10,139 kilometers) of roadways are paved. Interstate 95 connects Rhode Island with Massachusetts in the northeast and Connecticut in the southwest. Interstate 195 provides a route from Providence to Cape Cod, Massachusetts; Interstate 295 bypasses the city of Providence, resulting in efficient commercial traffic.

COMMUNICATION

Benjamin Franklin's brother James began publishing Rhode Island's first newspaper, the *Rhode Island Gazette*, in 1732. In 1758, James's son, also named James Franklin, founded yet another Rhode Island newspaper, the *Newport Mercury*. After 176 years of circulation, the *Mercury* was merged with the *Newport News*. It now appears as a weekly edition entitled *Newport Mercury and Weekly News*.

Today Rhode Island publishes about thirty newspapers, some daily and some weekly. The *Providence Journal* and the *Providence Evening Bulletin*, both published by the Providence Journal-Bulletin, are the state's most widely read papers.

Five television stations broadcast in Rhode Island. These include stations carrying the major national television networks, as well as the state department of education's public television station. About twenty-five AM and FM radio stations serve the state's listening audiences. A few of them are nonprofit stations operated by high-school and college students and broadcast from their campuses.

Chapter 8
ARTS AND RECREATION

ARTS AND RECREATION

PERFORMING ARTS

Rhode Island has a thriving performing-arts community of dancers, actors, singers, and instrumentalists. Concertgoers can find whatever suits their taste, whether it be classical, popular, or folk entertainment.

Providence's Rhode Island Philharmonic Orchestra has received glowing reviews all over the country. Talented young people perform in the Philharmonic-sponsored Rhode Island Youth Orchestra. Audiences can hear internationally acclaimed soloists in performances of the Providence Opera Theatre, the Rhode Island Civic Chorale and Orchestra, and the Performing Arts Association. Brown University, Rhode Island College, the University of Rhode Island, Rhode Island School of Design, and Salve Regina College present orchestral, choral, and solo concerts throughout the school year. In addition, the Young People's Symphony of Rhode Island offers several performances a season.

The Peloquin Chorale performs sacred and secular choral music in Providence's Saints Peter and Paul Cathedral and on national concert tours. On a lighter note, one can hear the all-male Society for the Preservation and Encouragement of Barbershop Quartet Singing in America, often performing with the all-female Melody Belles.

Musicians at a Newport music festival

In Newport, the summer air is filled with music. The Newport Music Festival, Newport Folk Festival, and Newport Jazz Festival draw audiences from all over the world.

Classical, modern, and folk dance are well represented in Rhode Island. The best-known ensembles are the State Ballet of Rhode Island, Festival Ballet of Rhode Island, Rhode Island Dance Repertory Company, and Helen O'Neill's Newport County Ballet Theatre. Other notable companies are Brown University's Festival Dancers, its Folk Dance Club, the Rhode Island College Dance Company, and the English Country Dancers.

Community theater in Rhode Island is a long-standing tradition. The Players, based in Providence, is the oldest community theater in the country. The capital city is also home to the Rhode Island Shakespeare Theatre; the Scitamard Players, a black theater company; and the Parish House Players. The Newport Players Guild and Naval War College Footlighters

Rhode Island's renowned cultural institutions include Trinity Square Repertory Company (left) and the Museum of Art at the Rhode Island School of Design (right).

entertain theatergoers in Newport. Numerous other community-theater groups take to the stage elsewhere around the state.

Professional theater flourishes in Rhode Island as well. Since it was founded in 1962, the Trinity Square Repertory Company has earned many prestigious honors. In 1968, it was the first American theater group ever invited to the distinguished Edinburgh Festival in Scotland. In 1981, the group won the Antoinette Perry ("Tony") Award for outstanding regional theater.

MUSEUMS

Many of Rhode Island's art, history, and natural-history museums tell fascinating stories of the state's past. Relics from

Rhode Island's glorious maritime days are on display in the Herreshoff Marine Museum in Bristol and the Museum of Yachting in Newport. Also in Newport is the Naval War College Museum, with exhibits on the history of war at sea.

The Roger Williams Park Museum of Natural History also has a maritime connection. Many of its artifacts from the South Pacific were brought back by Providence's nineteenth-century merchant ships. The museum also displays collections of shells, minerals, Indian artifacts, fossils, and mounted birds. Its planetarium is the only one in Rhode Island that is open to the public.

Brown University's Haffenreffer Museum of Anthropology, in Bristol, exhibits artifacts and other cultural items belonging to the early native peoples of North, Central, and South America, as well as Africa, Asia, the Middle East, and Oceania.

Rhode Island's art museums feature works by artists known locally, nationally, and internationally. The Museum of Art of the Rhode Island School of Design, in Providence, is one of New England's finest art museums. Besides an excellent collection of nineteenth- and twentieth-century French paintings and sculptures, the museum houses ancient Egyptian, Asian, Greek, and Roman pieces. Brown University's David Winton Bell Gallery has changing exhibits of prints, drawings, and photographs, as well as twentieth-century American paintings and sculptures. The art of Newport and New England is the focus of the Newport Art Museum and Art Association. In Pawtucket, the Rhode Island Watercolor Society exhibits works of its members. It also sponsors an occasional exchange show, such as its 1985 exchange exhibit with the Japan Watercolor Society.

Historical societies in Providence and Newport preserve homes and documents from Rhode Island's early days. In Providence, the Rhode Island Historical Society maintains the John Brown House,

The Providence Athenaeum is one of Rhode Island's many distinguished libraries.

called "one of the ten great houses in America." The society also owns the Museum of Rhode Island History at Aldrich House, which features an excellent library and exhibits covering the state's 350-plus years of history.

The Newport Historical Society houses archives, a library, and a museum. Among its holdings are early town records, letters and diaries, ancestry records, historic photographs, and early home furnishings. The society also maintains the 1675 Wanton-Lyman-Hazard House and the 1699 Friends' Meeting House and sponsors walking tours of historic Newport. The Preservation Society of Newport County preserves and offers tours through several of Newport's grand mansions.

Slater Mill Historic Site in Pawtucket, the birthplace of America's Industrial Revolution, includes Slater's textile mill, Wilkinson's waterwheel-powered machine shop, and the

Sylvanus Brown House. Also in Pawtucket is the Children's Museum of Rhode Island. There, children may play on the giant Rhode Island map on the floor, paint on easels, or putter in Great Grandmother's Kitchen.

At South County Museum in Narragansett, visitors can touch and work with the exhibits. An operating letterpress print shop is on the premises, as well as farm tools, spinning wheels and looms, vehicles, and toys from Rhode Island's earlier days.

Other Rhode Island museums include the Museum of Primitive Cultures in Peace Dale, the Betsey Williams Cottage in Providence, and the Westerly Museum and Art Gallery.

LIBRARIES

Rhode Islanders have had their own libraries for nearly three hundred years. The colony's first library was established in 1700 in Newport by Reverend Thomas Bray. Today, Newport's Redwood Library and Athenaeum, founded in 1747, is the state's oldest operating library.

As one might guess, many of Rhode Island's libraries contain historical collections. Brown University's John Hay Library, named after Abraham Lincoln's secretary, holds 11,000 Lincoln-related documents, 800 of them with Lincoln's signature. The campus's John Carter Brown Library, founded in 1846, is the world's foremost library of books about the Americas published before 1800.

Rhode Island and New England history are the focus at the Rhode Island Historical Society Library in Providence. Besides housing the largest collection of Rhode Island newspapers in the world, it contains 150,000 books, more than 1,000 journals, 300,000 images, and 3 million feet of film.

New England's second-largest library, the Providence Public Library, includes special collections on whaling, architecture, printing, Irish culture, and the Civil War. In the Rhode Island School of Design Library are more than 43,000 books on art, architecture, graphic design, photography, and apparel design. The Greek-Doric-style Providence Athenaeum, one of the first libraries in the country, holds many rare books. Also in Providence are the Rhode Island Regional Library for the Blind and Physically Handicapped and the Rhode Island School for the Deaf Library.

WRITERS AND ENTERTAINERS

Many renowned writers and entertainers were born in or lived in Rhode Island. One of the most famous is Providence-born H. P. Lovecraft, whose bizarre novels and short stories combine historical fact with haunting fantasies. A number of Rhode Island writers have been awarded the Pulitzer Prize for their literary works. Edwin O'Connor of Woonsocket received the prize in 1962 for his novel *The Edge of Sadness*. Poet Leonard Bacon of Peace Dale won the award in 1941. The novel *Laughing Boy*, by Christopher La Farge of South County, earned the prize in 1929.

Pawtucket native and Brown University graduate Irving R. Levine is one of the state's most distinguished natives. A longtime correspondent for the National Broadcasting Company, Levine also authored the book *Main Street, U.S.S.R.*

Rhode Island's best-known and best-loved entertainer was George M. Cohan—singer, dancer, composer, actor, playwright, and producer of musical comedies. Claiming in one of his songs to be a "Yankee Doodle Dandy, born on the Fourth of July," he was actually born on July 3, 1878, in Providence. With patriotic songs

Left: Windsurfing off Newport
Above: Freshwater fishing on Block Island

like "Over There" and "You're a Grand Old Flag," Cohan helped Americans through World War I. He is the only composer ever to receive the Congressional Medal of Honor.

OUTDOOR RECREATION

With hundreds of miles of waterfront, Rhode Island is richly endowed with boating, fishing, swimming, surfing, and skin-diving opportunities. Around eighty-five marinas, twenty-eight yacht clubs, and thirty major boating harbors serve those who ply the waters of the Atlantic Ocean and Narragansett Bay.

Saltwater fishing yields white marlin, bluefin tuna, broadbill swordfish, and many other game fish. In freshwater lakes and streams are trout, perch, smallmouth bass, and pike. Fishing tournaments abound. Off Rhode Island's shores are tournaments

A public beach in Narragansett

for catching tuna, shark, billfish, striped bass, and bluefish, among others.

Many of Rhode Island's thirty-three state parks are historic sites, wildlife refuges, or combinations of the two. They include Arcadia Management Area, Block Island National Wildlife Refuge, Burlingame State Park, Fort Adams State Park, and Roger Williams Park. In parks and in the state's many campgrounds, people enjoy picnicking, camping, golfing, horseback riding, hiking, and many other activities.

Besides state parks, Rhode Island also maintains state beaches. Along the coasts are forty-one public saltwater beaches and twenty-two public freshwater beaches. A number of private clubs and organizations have private beaches as well.

SAILING

Claiming to be the sailing capital of the world, Newport is host to a number of yacht races and regattas. Intrepid sailors and

Newport has been called the sailing capital of the world.

cheering fans pour into Newport every summer for the Volvo
Newport Regatta, the Maxi Races, the Newport Unlimited Regatta,
the Classic Yacht Regatta, and the Newport-to-Bermuda Races, to
name a few.

For fifty-three years, from 1930 to 1983, Newport was the home
of the America's Cup race, the most prestigious of all international
sailing competitions. The country that wins the cup is the host
country for the following race. Americans took the prize for an
incredible 132 years, from 1851 to 1983. Newporter Harold
Vanderbilt was one of the yachtsmen who helped keep the cup in
American hands for what has been called the longest winning
streak in sporting history. Bristol's Herreshoff Manufacturing
Company, founded in 1863 by a twenty-two-year-old blind

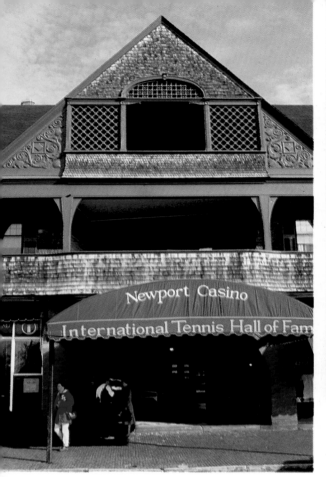

Newport is the site of the International Tennis Hall of Fame (left) and several professional tennis championships (above).

boatbuilder named John Brown Herreshoff, built more America's Cup winners than any other boat maker.

Amateur sailors and boaters also take advantage of the Ocean State's recreational waterways. During months of good weather, thousands of Rhode Islanders take to the water in their small sailing craft or outboard motorboats.

TENNIS

With more than a dozen tennis clubs and many public tennis courts, Rhode Island is an ideal spot for tennis buffs. The Newport Casino, a national historic landmark, now houses the International Tennis Hall of Fame. Home of the world's largest tennis museum, the grass-courted estate hosted the first national lawn tennis championship in 1881.

Newport is also the scene of the annual Volvo and Virginia Slims tennis championships. In addition, the city hosts the Men's and Women's National Amateur Grass Court Championships and the Women's National Professional Grass Court Championships.

TEAM SPORTS

At McCoy Stadium in Pawtucket, from April through September, baseball is truly "the only game in town." McCoy is the home stadium for the PawSox, as the Pawtucket Red Sox are most often called. The popular team is the Boston Red Sox's Class AAA International Baseball League affiliate. A hefty 60 percent of all PawSox players move up to the major leagues, most of them to the Boston Red Sox. Roger Clemens, Wade Boggs, and Mike Greenwell are just a few of the former PawSoxes who have gone on to major-league fame.

Rhode Island football fans can enjoy a summertime taste of their favorite wintertime sport. In July and August, the National Football League's New England Patriots hold training sessions at Bryant College in Smithfield. The Patriots' regular-season home games are in Foxboro, Massachusetts, only a half-hour's drive from Providence. Loyal college football fans cheer their favorite local teams at Providence College, the University of Rhode Island, and Brown University.

College basketball draws enthusiastic crowds to the Providence Civic Center every season. There they can see the Providence College Friars, members of the Big East Conference; the University of Rhode Island Rams, of the Atlantic Ten Conference; and Brown University's Ivy League team.

Chapter 9

A TOUR OF THE OCEAN STATE

A TOUR OF THE OCEAN STATE

PROVIDENCE

Up the steep, grassy slopes of Smith Hill is the State House, Rhode Island's state capitol building. This glistening edifice of white Georgian marble is topped by the second-largest self-supporting marble dome in the world. (The largest is the dome of St. Peter's Basilica in Rome, Italy.) Atop the dome, symbolizing Rhode Island's commitment to religious freedom, is a gilded statue of the Independent Man. Inside the spacious capitol are the 1663 Rhode Island colony charter and a full-length portrait of George Washington by Rhode Islander Gilbert Stuart.

A few blocks to the south is Kennedy Plaza, Providence's central square. Marking the center of the plaza is Bajnotti Fountain, a magnificent bronze work cast by Providence's Gorham Manufacturing Company.

The Arcade, at the east end of Weybosset Street, has the distinction of being the nation's oldest indoor shopping center. Built in 1828, this majestic piece of Greek Revival architecture is a national historic landmark. Inside, massive columns support the roof, while sunlight streams in upon three levels of shops, boutiques, and restaurants.

Southwest of the downtown area, with entrances at Elmwood Avenue and Broad Street, is Roger Williams Park. In 1871, Betsey

Thayer Street, near
Brown University
on Providence's
East Side, is lined
with a delightful
array of shops and
restaurants.

Williams, the great-great-great-granddaughter of Roger Williams,
donated her farm to the city of Providence, intending it to be
made into a park in honor of her famous ancestor. Today, it is a
420-acre (170-hectare) recreation area with ponds, winding
pathways, a Japanese garden, a greenhouse, tennis courts, a
natural-history museum, and a zoo.

PROVIDENCE'S EAST SIDE

Across the Providence River is the city's historic district, the
East Side. On the north end of the district, at Smith Street and
North Main, is Roger Williams National Memorial. This park is
the site where Roger Williams founded the Providence settlement

Roger Williams Park in Providence

in 1636. The spring from which he and his followers drew their water is here, too, although it is now an empty well.

Clustered along the hillside to the south of the park are lovingly preserved homes and public buildings from Rhode Island's earliest days. Benefit Street, called the "Mile of History," runs the length of the East Side. Using Benefit Street as a base, one can easily walk to the many historic buildings in the district.

At Angell and North Main streets is the First Baptist Meeting House. Topped by a 185-foot (56-meter) steeple, this church once housed the nation's first Baptist congregation, founded by Roger Williams in 1638. An active congregation still worships there today, and Brown University holds its commencement exercises there every spring.

A block south on Benefit Street is the Museum of Art of the Rhode Island School of Design. One of the finest small art museums in the country, it is noted for its French and American paintings and its American furniture collection.

Climbing up the steep hill from Benefit Street, one comes upon picturesque Brown University. Its oldest building, University Hall, was a hospital and barracks for French and American troops during the American Revolution. Down the hill once again from Brown is the stately Providence Athenaeum. In this library, which holds an impressive collection of rare books, poet Edgar Allan Poe courted Benefit Street resident Sarah Helen Whitman.

Travelers who visit the eastern United States are often amused to see plaques in taverns, inns, and boardinghouses announcing that "George Washington slept here." The Stephen Hopkins House, west of Benefit on Hopkins Street, boasts that Washington slept there twice! Hopkins, who signed the Declaration of Independence and was governor of Rhode Island for ten terms, lived in this 1707 clapboard home. Visitors may tour the home and also stroll, as Hopkins once did, through his lovely colonial garden.

Another few blocks down Benefit Street is the elegant 1786 mansion of merchant John Brown. Having opened up Providence's trade with China, Brown positioned his home so that he could gaze down upon the bustling waterfront below. The restored brick abode was, according to President John Quincy Adams, "the most magnificent and elegant private mansion that I have ever seen on this continent."

To the east, on Benevolent Street, is the Museum of Rhode Island History at Aldrich House. Once the home of United States Senator Nelson W. Aldrich, it exhibits documents and artifacts from Rhode Island's rich historical past.

Newport is a charming historic city at the southern tip of Aquidneck Island.

NEWPORT

About 20 miles (32 kilometers) south of Providence, Route 138 runs eastward to become the Jamestown Bridge. Within a few minutes, Newport-bound travelers cross Jamestown's Conanicut Island and ascend the Newport Bridge. This 2.5-mile (4-kilometer) bridge is the longest expansion bridge in the United States.

A peninsula off the southern tip of Aquidneck Island, Newport lies right in the center of the mouth of Narragansett Bay. Long famous as a summer resort for the super-rich, Newport is also known as the sailing capital of the world. Today, pleasure boats and million-dollar yachts jostle one another in the same harbor where merchant sailing ships once moved rum, molasses, and slaves. Granite cobblestone blocks, once used to give ships weight and balance, now pave many of Newport's streets.

Sloping up from the waterfront is Newport's oldest historic district. A good starting point for a walking tour of the area is

The White Horse Tavern (left) and the old Colony House (above) are two renowned Newport landmarks.

Washington Square, the center of colonial Newport's commercial and political activities. Here troops were drilled, slaves auctioned, and proclamations read. At the head of Washington Square is the old Colony House, a 1739 red-brick structure that served as one of Rhode Island's two state capitols until 1900. Colonial Newport's central market, Brick Market, stands at the foot of the square. Now filled with boutiques and eateries, it once received wagonloads of produce and other goods through its high-arched doorways.

Up the hill to the east is White Horse Tavern, now a restaurant, but famous as the oldest tavern building in the country. It was in 1687 that a private named William Mayes first obtained a liquor license for the premises. The White Horse sign was hung in 1730. Across Farewell Street is the 1699 Friends' Meeting House, America's oldest Quaker meeting place. The nearby Wanton-Lyman-Hazard House, built in 1675, is the oldest house in Newport. As the home of the British stamp master, it was almost torn down in 1765 by rioting colonists furious over the Stamp Act.

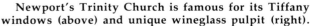
Newport's Trinity Church is famous for its Tiffany windows (above) and unique wineglass pulpit (right).

On Touro Street, built at an angle so that worshippers face Jerusalem, is Touro Synagogue. Dedicated in 1763, it is the oldest Jewish synagogue in North America. Five massive candelabra hang in the ornate but dignified interior. On one wall is a letter sent by George Washington to the congregation in 1790, assuring that "the Government of the United States . . . gives to bigotry no sanction, to persecution no assistance. . . ."

Trinity Church, at the head of Queen Anne Square, has Tiffany stained-glass windows and is topped by a graceful spire. Its triple-deck wineglass pulpit is the only such pulpit in the country. One of the church's box-style pews—number 81, to be exact—is famous. George Washington prayed there—not once, but often.

Days could be spent touring the many landmarks of colonial Newport. Other important buildings and sites in this area include Redwood Library, the Old Stone Mill, Hunter House, St. Mary's Church, and the Artillery Museum.

NEWPORT MANSIONS

No visitor should leave Newport without seeing the famous
Newport mansions, the summer homes of turn-of-the-century
captains of industry. In the short drive from the historic district to
the mansions, one passes Fort Adams State Park, where the
Newport jazz and folk festivals are held every summer. Just
beyond Fort Adams is Hammersmith Farm, the oceanside estate of
the Auchincloss family. When Mrs. Auchincloss's daughter,
Jacqueline Bouvier, married John F. Kennedy in 1953, the wedding
reception was held here. Later, during Kennedy's presidency, the
Kennedy family relaxed at Hammersmith many times.

Continuing along Newport's southern shore, one comes to
Ocean Drive, with its marvelous view of the rocky Atlantic
coastline. Extending up the eastern edge of the peninsula is Cliff
Walk, where hardy walkers can wind some 3 miles (5 kilometers)
up the coast. Bellevue and Ochre Point avenues, roughly parallel
to Cliff Walk, pass by many of Newport's stunning mansions.
Some of the mansions belong to private owners, while others
belong to the Preservation Society of Newport. Many have regular
visiting hours for the public.

The Breakers, the grandest of them all, was the summer home of
shipping magnate Cornelius Vanderbilt. Completed in 1895 and
built in less than three years, the seventy-room mansion is
modeled after an Italian villa. Another mansion, Marble House,
was a gift from William Vanderbilt, Cornelius's brother, to his
wife. Costing $11 million, it contains about 500,000 cubic feet
(14,159 cubic meters) of marble walls and columns.

Other mansions worth visiting are The Elms, summer home of
Pennsylvania coal king Edward Berwind; Chateau-sur-Mer, the
Victorian estate of China-trade merchant William Wetmore;

The Breakers (top left, top right), Marble House (bottom left), and Kingscote (bottom right) are among the many stunning Newport mansions that have been preserved and are open to the public.

Rosecliff, Mrs. Herman Oelrich's model of the Grand Trianon palace at Versailles in France; the Astors' Beechwood; Belcourt Castle; and Kingscote.

All the mansion owners were wealthy, and many were eccentric as well. The story is told that Oliver Hazard Perry Belmont, a bachelor who loved horses, kept several of them in his marble-floored Belcourt Castle—until he married. Then his wife insisted that the horses must go. Another Newport resident, it is said, once held an elegant dinner party for fifty dogs. She required the male dogs to wear tuxedos and the females to wear evening gowns. Her next-door neighbor disliked her so heartily that he had his hedges trimmed to resemble the British military—with their muskets pointed straight at his neighbor's mansion.

BEYOND NEWPORT

In the northern part of Aquidneck Island is Portsmouth, where Anne Hutchinson and her religious-refugee followers settled in 1638. There, on a 7-acre (2.8-hectare) country estate called Green Animals, are the famous topiary gardens of Miss Alice Brayton. Miss Brayton, who died in 1972 at the age of ninety-four, was fond of topiary, the art of hedge sculpturing. Now visitors can admire some eighty trees and shrubs that resemble such creatures as the giraffe, peacock, elephant, camel, and wild boar.

Back on the mainland north of Portsmouth is Bristol, situated on Mount Hope Bay. Here, Brown University's Haffenreffer Museum of Anthropology displays artifacts of the native peoples of North and South America, as well as Africa, Asia, Oceania, and the Middle East. Nearby, at the Herreshoff Marine Museum, one can see a fascinating collection of sailing vessels, ships' fittings, and cruise souvenirs.

Also in Bristol are the Blithewold Gardens and Arboretum. These 33 acres (13 hectares) overlooking Narragansett Bay include a bamboo grove, a giant sequoia tree, and many exotic plants.

The easternmost part of Rhode Island, attached to the Massachusetts mainland, is called the Sakonnet Lands. A major attraction here is the Sakonnet Vineyards in Little Compton. Visitors may walk through the vineyards, tour the winery, taste samples, or enjoy a picnic on the lawn.

SOUTH COUNTY

Officially named Washington County, the lower one-third of Rhode Island's mainland is better known as South County. Once the home of the Narragansett Indians, South County is a land of forests, beaches, and quaint harbor towns.

South of Wickford is the birthplace of portrait artist Gilbert Stuart. Both the colonial home and the snuff mill of the Stuart family are open to the public. A few miles away is the Silas Casey Farm, a typical farm from Rhode Island's plantation days.

Narragansett Pier, farther down the southeast coast, was once an elegant resort. A fire in 1900 destroyed its casino, but the town remains a charming seaport village with fishermen, old cottages, and the state's most popular beach. On South County's southeastern tip is Galilee, another quaint fishing village. Just west of here is Matunuck, home of the famous Theatre-By-The-Sea. Stage and screen stars have been appearing here since 1933.

From Point Judith, down the road from Galilee, visitors can take a ferry 10 miles (16 kilometers) south to Block Island, officially named New Shoreham. Visitors can walk or rent bicycles and ride to the island's points of interest. Around its northernmost tip, called Sandy Point, is the Block Island National Wildlife Refuge

Main Street on Block Island

and the Old North Light lighthouse. Nearby are Settlers' Cove, where colonists landed in 1662; and Cow Cove, where a cow that swam from a wrecked ship scrambled ashore. On the southeast end of the island are Mohegan Bluffs, looming 200 feet (61 meters) above a rugged beach.

Back on the mainland, a dozen or more public beaches line the southern coast. Route 1 runs along this coast as well, and from it one can reach South County's many wildlife refuges and ponds. South Kingstown's Great Swamp Fight Monument, a towering stone marker, commemorates those who died there in the Great Swamp Fight of 1675. In the Great Swamp Management Area, footpaths wind through bushes and trees where mink, raccoon, hawks, pheasants, and other wild species live.

In Charlestown, west of South Kingstown, is the Long House, the tribal headquarters of the Narragansett Indians. Here they practice many of their traditional crafts and hold an annual

Watch Hill is a lovely Victorian seaside resort in southwestern Rhode Island.

meeting. Also in Charlestown is Burlingame State Park, where swimmers can take a dip in Watchaug Pond.

In Westerly, Rhode Island's southwesternmost town, is the Victorian seaside resort of Watch Hill. Overlooking the water from a hillside are cottages and beach hotels. Closer to the waterfront, visitors may stroll past rows of restaurants and shops. At the entrance to Watch Hill Beach is the famous Flying Horse Carousel. Built in about 1879, this merry-go-round with its brightly painted horses is thought to be the oldest in the country.

THE BLACKSTONE VALLEY

Graced with waterfalls and swift currents, the Blackstone River is a vital part of Rhode Island's industrial history. Waterfalls throughout the valley—some natural and others created by damming—drove the massive waterwheels that powered its mills

A textile
mill in
Pawtucket

and factories. To get jobs here, thousands of immigrants poured
into the valley in the nineteenth century.

Rising in Massachusetts, the Blackstone cuts across Rhode
Island's northeast quadrant and becomes the Pawtucket River and
the Seekonk River before emptying into Narragansett Bay. In
1986, Congress established the Blackstone River Valley National
Heritage Corridor to preserve the waterways and historic
structures along the valley. The corridor stretches from Worcester,
Massachusetts, to Pawtucket, Rhode Island, and cuts through the
municipalities of Woonsocket, Cumberland, Lincoln, and
Pawtucket.

At the height of its industrial days, Woonsocket was largely
populated by French-Canadians. Many of their descendants
remain there today, and French is the city's second language.
Woonsocket's AutumnFest, held every October in World War II
Memorial State Park, features races, sports events, fireworks, and

a parade. Diamond Hill State Park, in nearby Cumberland, is an enjoyable spot for fishing, hiking, and picnicking. Throughout the summer, visitors can also enjoy the park's Sunday classical, jazz, rock, and country-western concerts.

Farther downriver is Pawtucket, called the "cradle of American industry." American manufacturers of textiles, anchors, tools, gears, spinning wheels, and a myriad of other goods were born in this bustling little town on the Blackstone River. The name *Pawtucket* itself is an Algonquian Indian word for "place of rushing water."

At the Slater Mill Historic Site in Pawtucket, visitors can tour two fascinating mills and a mill owner's home. Guides at the 1793 Slater Mill show how machines at each stage of the textile milling process turned raw cotton into thread. Beginning with a cotton gin for removing seeds, the tour ends with a machine that knits cotton thread into T-shirt fabric!

The 8-ton (7-metric ton) waterwheel at Wilkinson Mill powers all the gears in its second-story machine shop. In this amazing 1810 factory, visitors can watch lathes, drills, gear cutters, milling machines, and saws in action—just as they were almost two centuries ago. And all this spinning and whirling is powered by the waterwheel's steady creaking and clanking revolutions.

Nearby, in mill owner Sylvanus Brown's 1758 home, visitors can watch women spinning and hand-loom weaving the way women did two hundred years ago.

INLAND RHODE ISLAND

Western and central Rhode Island are more sparsely populated than the areas nearer the ocean and the bay. Still, among the

Autumn in Cumberland

inland forests, hills, rivers, and ponds are many enjoyable spots for recreation and relaxation.

The Arcadia Management Area, a massive state park, sprawls through Exeter, West Greenwich, Hopkinton, and Richmond. Right in the center of the state is Scituate Reservoir. Rhode Island's largest inland body of water, it gives Providence its water supply and fishermen a generous freshwater catch.

West of Scituate Reservoir, near the Connecticut border, is Jerimoth Hill, the state's highest point. More wildlife refuges lie to the north. One is the George Washington Management Area, adjoining Casimir Pulaski State Park. In the far northwestern corner of the state is Buck Hill Management Area, and a few miles to the east is Black Hut Management Area.

It is said that no point in Rhode Island is more than a forty-five-minute drive from Providence. This is good news for travelers. It gives them more time to explore the historical riches and natural beauties of the Ocean State.

FACTS AT A GLANCE

GENERAL INFORMATION

Statehood: May 29, 1790, thirteenth state

Official Name: State of Rhode Island and Providence Plantations

Origin of Name: The origin of the name *Rhode Island* is disputed. According to one theory, the name arose from a description by Giovanni da Verrazano. After coming upon Block Island in 1524, the navigator wrote that it was "about the size of the island of Rhodes," a Greek island in the Aegean Sea. Others trace the name's origin to Adriaen Block. Discovering an island in Narragansett Bay in 1614, the Dutch explorer called it *Roodt Eylandt*, meaning "red island," because of its red clay soil. Whatever its origins, the name *Rhode Island* was eventually given to Aquidneck Island, the largest island in Narragansett Bay and the site of the Portsmouth and Newport settlements. Rhode Island's first colonial settlement, however, was on the mainland. Roger Williams named the settlement *Providence* in 1636 in gratitude for God's providence in bringing him and his followers safely through the wilderness on their flight from Massachusetts. The first (1644) charter for this colony of farmers was issued to "the Providence Plantations in Narragansett Bay." By 1663, when Rhode Island's second charter was issued, the settlement on the Island of Rhode Island had grown in importance. The new charter called the colony "Rhode Island and Providence Plantations," and the state has retained that lengthy title.

State Capital: Providence, founded 1636

State Nickname: Ocean State; also called Little Rhody

State Flag: Rhode Island adopted its state flag in 1897, the third of the original thirteen colonies to adopt an official flag. The flag's white background symbolizes the Rhode Island soldiers who lost their lives in the American Revolution. In the center of the flag is a gold anchor, symbolizing hope, surrounded by thirteen gold stars representing the thirteen original colonies. Under the anchor is a blue ribbon on which is inscribed the word *hope* in gold letters. By state law, the flag is to be edged with a gold fringe, and its flagstaff is to be topped by a spearhead.

State Motto: "Hope"

State Bird: Rhode Island Red chicken

State Shell: Quahog

State Flower: Violet

State Tree: Red maple

State Mineral: Bowenite

State Stone: Cumberlandite

State Song: "Rhode Island," words and music by T. Clarke Brown, adopted as the state song in 1946:

> Here's to you, belov'd Rhode Island,
> With your Hills and Ocean Shore,
> We are proud to hail you "Rhody"
> And your Patriots of yore.
> First to claim your Independence,
> Rich your heritage and fame,
> The smallest State, smallest State
> and yet so great, so great,
> We will glorify your name.

POPULATION

Population: 947,154, fortieth among the states (1980 census)

Population Density: 780 people per sq. mi. (301 per km²)

Population Distribution: 87 percent of the people live in urban areas, with about 65 percent living in the Providence metropolitan area.

Providence	156,804
Warwick	87,123
Cranston	71,992
Pawtucket	71,204
East Providence	50,980
Woonsocket	45,914
Newport	29,259
North Providence	29,188

(Population figures according to the 1980 census)

Population Growth: Rhode Island's population growth has been closely tied to its economic conditions. The introduction of waterpowered manufacturing in 1790 brought a flood of immigrants into the state to work in its factories and mills. Between 1800 and 1850, the state's population more than doubled. With the continued growth of manufacturing and new waves of immigrants, the 1910 population figure almost quadrupled the 1850 count. The closing of textile mills in the 1920s, coupled with unemployment during the Great Depression of the 1930s, caused many residents to leave the state in search of jobs. Rhode Island's population growth during the entire decade of the 1930s was a mere 3.8 percent.

The Wickford Art Festival is one of New England's oldest and largest art fairs.

Census figures rose steadily through the 1940s, 1950s, and 1960s. In the 1970s, however, the state registered a drop in population for the first time in its history. The decline was partly due to the closing of U.S. Navy installations in the state.

Year	Population
1790	68,825
1800	69,122
1820	83,059
1840	108,830
1860	174,620
1880	276,531
1900	428,556
1920	604,397
1930	687,497
1940	713,346
1950	791,896
1960	859,488
1970	949,723
1980	947,154

GEOGRAPHY

Borders: Connecticut lies along Rhode Island's western border, and Massachusetts lies to the north and east. The Atlantic Ocean forms Rhode Island's southern boundary, except for the span where Narragansett Bay cuts into the state.

Highest Point: Jerimoth Hill, 812 ft. (247 m)

Lowest Point: Sea level, along the Atlantic Ocean

Block Island is a beautiful, quiet resort that lies a few miles off the southern coast of the Rhode Island mainland.

Greatest Distances: North to south—48 mi. (77 km)
East to west—37 mi. (60 km)

Area: 1,214 sq. mi. (3,144 km²)

Rank in Area Among the States: Fiftieth

Rivers: Rhode Island's major rivers are the Pawtucket, Blackstone and Seekonk, Providence, Moshassuck, Woonasquatucket, and Pawcatuck. Others are the Pettaquamscutt, Sakonnet, Chepachet, Kickemuit, Moosup, Ponaganset, Queen, Wood, Tenmile, and Warren. While most of the rivers are freshwater, three are saltwater estuaries of Narragansett Bay: the Providence, Sakonnet, and Seekonk. Mount Hope Bay and Greenwich Bay are also saltwater extensions of the bay. The Blackstone River drops several hundred feet in elevation between its head in Massachusetts and its mouth in Narragansett Bay, resulting in a number of natural waterfalls along its course. Because of a general decline in elevation from the inlands to the coastal areas, many of the state's other rivers are also graced by waterfalls. Before the Blackstone River reaches the bay, its name changes to the Pawtucket and finally to the Seekonk River. The north branch of the Pawtucket River opens into the massive Scituate Reservoir in central Rhode Island. In the southwestern part of the state, the Pawtucket River forms part of the Connecticut-Rhode Island border.

Lakes: Rhode Island has nearly 300 reservoirs, lakes, and ponds. The largest inland body of water in the state is Scituate Reservoir. Including the waters of its five tributaries, the Scituate contains more than 41 billion gal. (155 billion l) of water. Other sizable bodies of water are Watchaug Pond, Ninigret Pond, Quonochontaug Pond, and Point Judith Pond—all along the state's southern lowlands.

Topography: Geographers divide Rhode Island into two major land areas: the Coastal Lowlands and the Eastern New England Upland. The Coastal Lowlands cover more than half the state's land area and are part of the coastal lowland region that extends along the entire New England coast. Rhode Island's Coastal Lowlands include the islands in Narragansett Bay, the lands east of the bay, and the coasts and coastal plains in the south and along the eastern part of the mainland. The southern coast is characterized by sandy beaches, salt ponds, marshes, and lagoons. On the islands and along the shores of the bay are rocky promontories and cliffs. Hills east of the bay are gently rounded and lightly wooded, while those west of the bay are more craggy and tend to be heavily forested. Farther into the mainland, these hills rise in elevation.

The Eastern New England Upland covers the state's inland areas to the north and west. It is part of an upland region that sweeps from Maine down to Connecticut. The valleys and sloping hills of Rhode Island's uplands rise steadily in elevation from the east to the west. In the northwest and west-central regions of the state are its highest elevations. Rhode Island's highest point, Jerimoth Hill, is on the far western edge of the state, next to the Connecticut border.

Climate: Rhode Island's climate is temperate and mild. The state's predominant weather influences come from the land to the northwest, west, and southwest. Breezes from the Atlantic Ocean and Narragansett Bay, however, cool the summer's heat and moderate the winter's chill. Snowstorms, for instance, tend to drop their moisture on Rhode Island in the form of rain instead of snow. The state's most severe weather features are hurricanes, tidal waves, and other coastal storms, with late summer and early fall the most likely times for these disasters. The hurricane of 1938 devastated much of the coastal region. Other major hurricanes struck the state in 1815, 1869, 1944, 1954, 1955, and 1960. A barrier across the Providence River to guard against future hurricane damage was completed by the U.S. Corp of Engineers in 1966.

The most pleasant weather occurs from April through June and from September through mid-November. January and February are the coldest months, with an average January temperature of 29° F. (-2° C). Kingston holds the record for the state's coldest recorded temperature, -23° F. (-30.5° C) on January 11, 1942. The hottest days usually fall in July and August, with the July temperature averaging 71° F. (22° C). The state's highest recorded temperature was 104° F. (40° C), registered in Providence on August 2, 1975.

About 44 in. (112 cm) of precipitation (rain, snow, and other moisture) falls on Rhode Island every year. Thunderstorms account for most of the state's precipitation in the spring and summer months. The average yearly snowfall is about 31 in. (79 cm), with the heaviest snows occurring in February. Because the coastal air tends to turn snow to rain, snowfall is heavier in the north and west than in the south and east.

NATURE

Trees: Ashes, beeches, birches, cedars, dogwoods, elms, hemlocks, hickories, red maples, oaks, pines, poplars, willows

Wild Plants: Asters, buttercups, cattails, daisies, ferns, goldenrod, lilies, milkweed, mountain laurels, orchids, red deer grass, scarlet pimpernels, rhododendron, seaweeds, sedges, trilliums, violets, wild carrots, wild roses

Animals: Beavers, foxes, hares, minks, moles, muskrats, opossums, otters, rabbits, raccoons, shrews, skunks, squirrels, white-tailed deer, woodchucks

Birds: Blue jays, catbirds, crows, eagles, falcons, flickers, ruffed grouse, gulls, hawks, loons, ospreys, barred owls, screech owls, partridges, pheasants, pigeons, quails, robins, sparrows, starlings, terns, wild ducks, woodcocks

Fish: Sea bass, striped bass, bluefish, cod, eel, flounder, mackerel, white marlin, menhaden, perch, pickerel, pike, scup, shark, squeteague, swordfish, trout, bluefin tuna

Shellfish: Soft-shell clams, blue crabs, lobsters, mussels, oysters, quahogs (hard-shell clams), scallops

GOVERNMENT

Like the nation's federal government, Rhode Island's state government is organized into three branches—legislative, executive, and judicial. The state legislature, or General Assembly, consists of a fifty-member senate and a one-hundred-member house of representatives. All members of the General Assembly are elected to two-year terms. The legislators make the state's laws, appoint justices to the state supreme court, and may override the governor's veto by a three-fifths vote.

The executive branch, headed by the governor, carries out the state's laws. Rhode Island's governor is elected to a two-year term and may serve for any number of terms. The other major executive officers are the lieutenant governor, attorney general, secretary of state, and general treasurer. With the approval of the state senate, the governor appoints the heads of twenty state government departments.

The state's judicial branch interprets the laws and tries cases. The state supreme court, consisting of a chief justice and four associate justices, is the state's highest court. All five members are elected by the General Assembly and serve for life. The supreme court is the highest court to which cases from lower state courts may be appealed. It also issues opinions on the constitutionality of measures passed by the General Assembly. The next level of state courts consists of the superior courts and family courts. Superior courts hear jury trials of criminal cases and those civil cases in which more than $5,000 is at stake. Family courts hold bench trials in divorce, child support, custody, adoption, and similar matters. District court judges are appointed by the governor, and probate judges are appointed by city and town councils.

Number of Counties: Rhode Island has five counties—Providence, Kent, Washington, Bristol, and Newport—but no county government. Instead, the state is divided into 39 municipalities, each of which has its own local government.

U.S. Representatives: 2

Electoral Votes: 4

Voting Qualifications: Citizen of the United States, at least eighteen years of age, thirty days residency

EDUCATION

In 1640, Robert Lenthal opened one of the first public schools in colonial America in Newport. Rhode Island continued to take a leading role in education, imposing America's first tax for the support of public schools in 1800. Today, Rhode Island's local communities spend more than half of their property-tax revenues on education.

The State Board of Regents oversees Rhode Island's public-school system, forms policies, and sets education standards. More than 134,000 students are enrolled in the state's forty public-school districts, at an average cost of $4,677 per student. Another 27,000 students attend parochial schools, and 2,600 attend other private schools. The average ratio between students and teachers in Rhode Island is fifteen to one. Children are required by law to attend school from age seven through age fifteen.

The state maintains three public institutions of higher learning: the University of Rhode Island, whose main campus is in Kingston; Rhode Island College in Providence, the second-oldest college in the state; and the Community College of Rhode Island, a two-year college with campuses in Warwick and Lincoln. The University of Rhode Island's oceanographic research facilities are among the finest in the country. The state's oldest college is Brown University in Providence. Brown, chartered in 1764, is New England's third-oldest college after Harvard and Yale and the seventh-oldest in the country. Also in Providence is the highly respected Rhode Island School of Design, offering training in art, design, and architecture. At Johnson and Wales University in Providence, students train for careers in the "hospitality industry"—hotels, motels, and restaurants. The U.S. Navy maintains its Naval War College in Newport. The Roman Catholic Dominican religious order operates Providence College. Another Catholic institution, Salve Regina College, is located in Newport. Other colleges in Rhode Island include Bryant College in Smithfield, Roger Williams College in Bristol, Hall Institute of Technology in Providence, and the New England Institute of Technology in Providence and Warwick.

ECONOMY AND INDUSTRY

Principal Products:

Agriculture: Nursery and greenhouse products, dairy products, poultry, eggs, hogs, potatoes, hay, sweet corn, tomatoes, snap beans, squash, cabbage, apples, peaches, pears, grapes, berries, wine

Manufacturing: Jewelry, silverware, fabricated metal products, electrical equipment, nonelectrical equipment, textiles, primary metals, printed materials, plastics products, rubber products, electronic equipment, instrumentation, chemicals, boats and ships, transportation equipment, food products

Natural Resources: granite, limestone, sandstone, coal, graphite, quartzite, iron, water, lumber, sand, gravel

Business and Trade: Although service industries provide the largest chunk of Rhode Island's gross state product (GSP) — 68 percent — the single-most-important economic activity in the state is manufacturing, accounting for about 27 percent of the GSP. Rhode Island leads the nation in production of both costume jewelry and sterling-silver products. Both industries had their beginnings in Rhode Island's colonial days.

Headquartered in Rhode Island are a number of large corporations. Textron, Inc., one of the nation's first business conglomerates, is based in Providence. Other major firms that have their headquarters in Rhode Island are Allied Aftermarket, Leviton, Davol, Raytheon, Amperex, Peterson Puritan, Brown and Sharpe, Amtrol, the New England regional office of Metropolitan Life Insurance Company, Hasbro, Allendale Insurance, Amica Insurance, Nortek, and Foster Parents Plan, Inc.

Communication: Rhode Island's publishers issue about 30 newspapers and 20 periodicals. Seven of the newspapers are published daily, while the majority are weekly publications. The Providence Journal-Bulletin's morning paper, the *Providence Journal*, and its evening edition, the *Providence Evening Bulletin*, have the highest circulation, followed by the *Pawtucket Times*, the *Woonsocket Call*, and the *Newport News*. The *Newport Mercury*, founded in 1758 by Benjamin Franklin's nephew James Franklin, exists today as the *Newport Mercury and Weekly News*, a weekly edition of the *Newport News*. The state's earliest newspaper was the *Rhode Island Gazette*, established in 1732 by Benjamin Franklin's brother James.

Providence's WJAR-TV was the state's first television station, beginning operation in 1949. Today, five television stations broadcast in the state. Three are affiliates of the nation's major networks, one is a public television station, and one is an affiliate of the Fox network. There are about 25 radio stations in Rhode Island, half of them FM stations and the rest AM or AM-FM. Although most of the state's radio stations are commercially operated, a few are nonprofit stations run by high-school and college students from their campuses.

Transportation: About 6,300 mi (10,139 km) of highways and roads crisscross the state, most of them paved. The completion of Rhode Island's segment of Interstate 95 in 1969 marked a definite increase in the state's tourism activity. The interstate provides for easy access to Rhode Island from Massachusetts on the northeast and Connecticut on the southwest. Other important highways are

The Providence Train Station in downtown Providence

Interstate 295, which bypasses Providence; Interstate 195, which runs from Rhode Island to Cape Cod, Massachusetts; Route 146, running from Providence to Woonsocket and on into Worcester, Massachusetts; and Route 1A, lining Rhode Island's southern shore.

The Theodore Francis Green State Airport in Warwick is the state's major airport, as well as southern New England's most important commercial air facility. General aviation airports are also located in Smithfield, Newport, Westerly, Block Island, and North Kingstown. An airport at the former Quonset Point Naval Air Station now serves the Rhode Island Air National Guard.

The Port of Providence, at the head of Narragansett Bay, is southern New England's major port of entry for its petroleum products. Fuel oil, gasoline, and kerosene, as well as automobiles, lumber, chemicals, and cement, are some of the goods unloaded there from incoming vessels. Rhode Island exports cargoes of scrap iron, manufactured goods, and other products from the Port of Providence. The Providence and Worcester Railroad is Rhode Island's major rail carrier. The Providence Train Station provides Amtrak service.

SOCIAL AND CULTURAL LIFE

Museums: Many cities and towns in Rhode Island have museums of art, history, or culture. Museums in Providence include the Museum of Rhode Island History at Aldrich House, which features exhibits on the state's cultural history. It is maintained by the Rhode Island Historical Society, which also maintains the John

The Redwood Library and Athenaeum in Newport is the state's oldest library.

Brown House, called "one of the ten great houses in America." The Rhode Island School of Design's Museum of Art exhibits French, Oriental, Greek, and Roman artworks, and its adjoining Pendleton House is an "American Wing" of early American home furnishings. RISD also maintains exhibits in its Woods-Gerry Gallery and Bayard Ewing Building. Brown University's David Winton Bell Gallery offers student, faculty, and traveling exhibits. At the Roger Williams Park Museum of Natural History are Indian artifacts, artifacts from the South Pacific, mounted birds, and a planetarium. Other Providence museums include the Betsey Williams Cottage and the Providence Art Club.

Newport is a treasure trove of historical museums. The Newport Historical Society houses archives, a library, and a museum with documents and artifacts from Newport's colonial days. The society also maintains the Wanton-Lyman-Hazard House and the Friends' Meeting House. The Preservation Society of Newport County preserves and gives tours through many of Newport's fabulous, turn-of-the-century mansions and other Newport historical buildings. Also in Newport are the Museum of Yachting and the Newport Art Museum and Art Association.

Pawtucket is the site of the Slater Mill Historic Site, the Children's Museum of Rhode Island, and the Rhode Island Watercolor Society. In Bristol are Brown University's Haffenreffer Museum of Anthropology and the Herreshoff Marine Museum. Narragansett's South County Museum displays machines and tools from Rhode Island's colonial days that visitors may touch and operate. Other museums in Rhode Island are the Warwick Museum in Warwick, the Museum of Primitive Cultures in Peace Dale, and the Westerly Museum and Art Gallery in Westerly.

Libraries: Rhode Island's Department of State Library Services, established in 1964, oversees state and federal funding for the state's libraries. There are about 50 public libraries, 20 libraries connected with colleges or universities, and 40 libraries devoted to social subjects in Rhode Island. Newport's Redwood Library and Athenaeum, founded in 1747, is the state's oldest library. The Providence Public Library, with seven branch libraries, is the second-oldest in New England. The Greek-Doric-style Providence Athenaeum is one of the oldest libraries in the country. Providence's Rhode Island State Library maintains a law collection, used by the state's government officials as well as by the public. Also in Providence, the Rhode Island Historical Society Library maintains books, journals, photographs, and film footage documenting Rhode Island and New England history. Brown University's John Hay Library houses the McLellan Lincoln Collection, the Webster Knight Stamp Collection, and the Harris Collection of American Poetry and Plays. The university's John Carter Brown Library, founded in 1846, contains many thousands of rare books and has the nation's foremost collection of books published about America before 1800. The Rhode Island School of Design Library contains more than 43,000 volumes on graphic design, art, architecture, and photography.

Performing Arts: The Rhode Island Philharmonic Symphony Orchestra is New England's second-most-popular orchestra, after the Boston Symphony. Other sources of fine classical music performances in Providence are the Providence Opera Theatre, the Rhode Island Civic Chorale and Orchestra, and the Performing Arts Association. Brown University presents the Rhode Island Chamber Music Concerts. Brown, the University of Rhode Island, the Rhode Island School of Design, and Salve Regina College all present orchestral, choral, and solo recitals throughout the year. Newport attracts music lovers to its classical, folk, and jazz festivals.

The Rhode Island State Ballet Company is one of the nation's most respected dance troupes. Harrisville's American Ballet and Brown University's dance companies present diverse and innovative repertoires. Other dance ensembles in the state are the Festival Ballet of Rhode Island, the Rhode Island Dance Repertory Company, Helen O'Neill's Newport County Ballet Theatre, the Rhode Island College Dance Company, and the English Country Dancers.

Rhode Island has an active theater community. The Trinity Square Repertory Company in Providence, a professional company, has received national and international acclaim. Alias Stage, an outgrowth of Trinity, produces original contemporary works. Providence also boasts the Rhode Island Shakespeare Theatre, the Second Story Theatre Company, the Players, the Scitamard Players, and the Parish House Players. The Theatre-By-The-Sea in Matunuck has brought famous stars to its stages for decades. Newport hosts the Newport Players Guild and the Naval War College Footlighters.

Sports and Recreation: Rhode Island is a haven for football, baseball, yachting, golf, and jai alai enthusiasts. Bryant College in Smithfield is the summer training ground for the National Football League's New England Patriots. The Pawtucket Red Sox, nicknamed the PawSox, are a Class AAA International Baseball League affiliate of the Boston Red Sox. The PawSox, who send about 60 percent of their

A private boat in Barrington at Christmastime

players on to the major leagues, play in Pawtucket's McCoy Stadium. College basketball fans enjoy the Providence College Friars, members of the Big East Conference; the University of Rhode Island Rams, of the Atlantic Ten Conference; and Brown University's Ivy League team.

Newport, called by some the yachting capital of the world, hosts the Volvo Newport Regatta, the Maxi Races, the Newport Unlimited Regatta, the Classic Yacht Regatta, the Newport-to-Bermuda Races, and many others. Until America lost to Australia in 1983, Newport had been the home of the prestigious America's Cup race 25 consecutive times. Newport, also home of the International Tennis Hall of Fame, hosts several annual tennis championships. The town of Barrington hosts the annual National Senior Women's Golf Tournament. Thousands of jai alai fans flock to Newport's Jai-Alai Sports Theatre to cheer their favorite teams.

Fishing, swimming, camping, and boating enthusiasts enjoy Rhode Island's 85 marinas, 28 yacht clubs, and 30 boating harbors; its 33 state parks and 63 state beaches; and its public fishing areas. Charlestown's Burlingame State Park is the state's major camping area. Popular saltwater beaches are maintained in Narragansett at Wheeler, Scarborough, and Galilee; in South Kingstown at East Matunuck; in Westerly at Misquamicut; in Warwick at Goddard Park; and in New Shoreham at Block Island State Beach. Major city parks are Roger Williams Park in Providence and Slater Park in Pawtucket.

The John Brown House, built in 1786, is now a fascinating museum maintained by the Rhode Island Historical Society.

Historic Sites and Landmarks:

Brick Market, at the foot of Newport's Washington Square, was built in 1762 as a warehouse and receiving house for goods being shipped in and out of Newport. Its Nostalgia Factory now displays old advertisements and other memorabilia.

John Brown House, in Providence, was designed by architect Joseph Brown in 1786 for his brother John. President John Quincy Adams called it "the most magnificent and elegant private mansion that I have ever seen on this continent."

Colony House, on Newport's Washington Square, is the second-oldest capitol building in the United States, built in 1739. It was the seat of colonial Rhode Island's British government, and then, until 1900, one of two meeting places for Rhode Island's General Assembly.

First Baptist Meeting House, in Providence, is the oldest Baptist church in America. Erected in 1775, the building has a 185-ft. (56-m) steeple and a massive Waterford crystal chandelier.

Friends Meeting House, in Newport, is the nation's oldest Quaker meetinghouse. First built in 1699, it has since been restored and houses models and architectural exhibits. Today it is the site of the New England Yearly Meeting of the Society of Friends.

Hunter House, in Newport, was built in 1748 and served as headquarters for Admiral de Ternay, commander of the French naval forces in America during the Revolutionary War.

Redwood Library, in Newport, is the nation's oldest library building in continuous use. Designed by architect Peter Harrison, it was built in 1748.

Roger Williams National Memorial, built around the site of colonial Providence's old town spring, commemorates Roger Williams's contribution to civil and religious liberties. Audiovisual presentations and displays at the visitor's center provide visitors with historical background on the site.

Royal Indian Burial Ground, in Charlestown, is the historic resting place of sachems (chiefs) and families of the Narragansett Indians.

Slater Mill Historic Site, in Pawtucket, commemorates the birth of America's Industrial Revolution through exhibits of crafts and working machinery. The site includes Slater Mill (1793), the nation's first water-driven cotton mill; the Sylvanus Brown House (1758); and the Wilkinson Mill (1810).

Gilbert Stuart Birthplace and Snuff Mill, near Wickford, dates from 1751. Visitors can view the famous portrait artist's birthplace, with many original home furnishings, as well as the family's snuff-making mill.

Touro Synagogue National Historic Site, in Newport, is the site of North America's oldest Jewish synagogue, dedicated in 1763. Designed by renowned architect Peter Harrison, it features Windsor benches and massive bronze candelabra. The adjacent cemetery was the inspiration for Henry Wadsworth Longfellow's poem "The Jewish Cemetery at Newport."

Trinity Church, in Newport, at the head of Queen Anne Square, was built in 1726. George Washington and philosopher George Berkeley worshipped there. Its triple-tiered wineglass pulpit is the only one of its kind in the nation.

Wanton-Lyman-Hazard House, in Newport, is the city's oldest house. Built in 1675 and home of the British stamp master in the pre-Revolutionary War period, it was severely damaged by rioting colonists in 1765 but has been restored to its former elegance.

Other Interesting Places to Visit:

The Arcade, in Providence, is the oldest indoor shopping center in America. Built in 1828, the magnificent Greek Revival structure is a bustling marketplace for international boutiques and eateries.

Green Animals Topiary Gardens in Portsmouth features trees and shrubs pruned into the shapes of animals.

Benefit Street, on Providence's East Side, is called the "Mile of History." Along this hilly district is one of America's most impressive arrays of colonial homes, many built in Federal, Georgian, and nineteenth-century architectural styles.

The Breakers, in Newport, was built in 1895 for Cornelius Vanderbilt. Modeled after sixteenth-century Italian villas and maintained by the Preservation Society of Newport County, the 70-room mansion is the most magnificent of Newport's celebrated turn-of-the-century summer homes.

Brown University, in Providence, is the seventh-oldest college in the country and the third-oldest in New England. Founded in 1764, the former Rhode Island College was renamed for Nicholas Brown after his generous endowment.

Great Swamp Fight Monument, in South Kingstown, is a stone obelisk memorializing the Narragansett and Wampanoag Indians who were massacred by colonial troops in December 1675 during King Philip's War. In the nearby Great Swamp Management Area are walking trails where one can see mink, raccoons, deer, hawks, owls, and other wildlife.

Green Animals Topiary Gardens, in Portsmouth, features 80 sculptured trees and shrubs that resemble such animals as giraffes, camels, peacocks, and wild boars. Formerly the gardens of topiary enthusiast Alice Brayton, they adjoin her home, now a children's museum featuring nineteenth-century toys and children's furniture.

Hammersmith Farm, in Newport, is Newport's only working farm. Built for the Auchincloss family in 1887, the 28-room cottage is now best known as having been a "summer White House" for President John F. Kennedy. He and his wife, Jacqueline, daughter of Mrs. Hugh Auchincloss, held their wedding reception there.

Stephen Hopkins House, built in Providence in 1707, was the home of Stephen Hopkins, signer of the Declaration of Independence and ten-time governor of Rhode Island. George Washington slept there twice.

Old Stone Mill, in Newport, is a circular tower of unknown origin. Some insist that it was built by Norsemen in the eleventh century. Henry Wadsworth Longfellow wrote of it in this vein in his ballad "Skeleton in Armor." Others say it was built in the 1600s by Rhode Island governor Benedict Arnold, grandfather of the famous traitor.

Sakonnet Vineyards, in Little Compton, grow the grapes from which Rhode Island's award-winning wines are made. From May through October, visitors may observe grape growing, harvesting, and wine making. They may also taste selected wines and picnic on the lawns.

State House, in Providence, is modeled after the U.S. Capitol in Washington, D.C. As a tribute to Rhode Island's history of religious freedom, a statue of the Independent Man stands atop the massive dome, the second-largest self-supporting marble dome in the world. Inside the white marble structure is the colony's 1663 charter and a full-length portrait of George Washington by Rhode Islander Gilbert Stuart.

IMPORTANT DATES

1524—Italian navigator Giovanni da Verrazano, sailing for France, explores Narragansett Bay

1614—Dutch navigator Adriaen Block lands on what is later named Block Island

1636—Roger Williams establishes Providence, Rhode Island's first settlement

1638—William Coddington, John Clarke, Anne Hutchinson, and others found Portsmouth on Aquidneck Island

1639—Roger Williams and Ezekiel Holliman found the Baptist Society of America in Providence (America's first Baptist church); Coddington and Clarke leave Portsmouth and found the town of Newport

1643 — Samuel Gorton establishes the town of Warwick after buying a piece of land, called Shawomet, from Miantonomi

1644 — Roger Williams obtains a charter from England for the Rhode Island colony

1647 — Providence, Portsmouth, Newport, and Warwick unite under the charter granted to Williams in 1644

1658 — Fifteen Sephardic Jewish families arrive in Newport and start a congregation

1663 — King Charles II grants the Rhode Island colony a second charter, providing for religious freedom and self-governance

1675 — During King Philip's War, settlers defeat Narragansett Indians in the Great Swamp Fight near Kingston

1696 — Newport's slave trade begins

1699 — Quakers in Newport set up America's first Quaker meetinghouse

1733 — Rhode Island shippers begin smuggling molasses into the colony after England passes the Molasses Act, restricting the importation of foreign molasses to the colonies

1739 — "War of Jenkins's Ear" begins when Spaniards seize the ship of Rhode Island smuggler Robert Jenkins and cut off Jenkins's ear; the resulting conflict becomes part of the War of Austrian Succession, known in the New World as King George's War

1754-63 — Rhode Island troops take part in the French and Indian War

1764 — Rhode Island College, later to become Brown University, is founded

1772 — Rhode Islanders burn the British revenue ship *Gaspee* to protest severe taxation

1774 — The importing of slaves is outlawed in Rhode Island; Stephen Hopkins and Samuel Ward represent Rhode Island at the First Continental Congress

1775 — Esek Hopkins is appointed commander-in-chief of the Continental navy

1776 — On May 4, two months before the Declaration of Independence, Rhode Island becomes the first colony to renounce allegiance to England; British forces occupy Newport

1778 — Rhode Island votes approval of the Articles of Confederation; in the Battle of Rhode Island, American and French troops battle the British in Newport

1781—Newport-based French troops begin marching toward Yorktown

1784—Rhode Island passes a law providing for the gradual abolition of slavery

1787—Rhode Islanders are forbidden by law to take part in the slave trade

1790—Rhode Island becomes a state when it ratifies the U.S. Constitution on May 29, the last of the thirteen colonies to do so; Moses Brown and Samuel Slater open the nation's first successful cotton textile mill in Pawtucket

1794—Providence silversmith Nehemiah Dodge perfects a way to plate base metals with precious metals, marking the beginning of Rhode Island's jewelry industry

1842—Thomas Dorr leads reform movement, known as the Dorr Rebellion, demanding fairer voting rights and legislative representation

1843—New state constitution, an amended version of which is still in effect today, expands voting rights

1883—U.S. Navy opens the Newport Naval Station

1884—Naval War College is established in Newport

1900—Providence officially becomes Rhode Island's capital

1935—Governor Theodore Francis Green reorganizes state government in what becomes known as the "Bloodless Revolution"

1938—A severe hurricane causes massive damage along the state's coasts

1941—U.S. Navy establishes Quonset Point Naval Air Station at Quonset Point near Davisville

1951—During a state constitutional convention, many new amendments are adopted, including one providing for home rule in cities and towns

1966—U.S. Corps of Engineers completes a hurricane barrier protecting Providence; Rhode Island legislature is reapportioned

1968—Rhode Island voters reject proposal for a new state constitution

1969—Newport Bridge, stretching across Narragansett Bay from Jamestown to Newport, is opened; Rhode Island's sector of Interstate 95 is completed

1971—Rhode Island General Assembly approves a state personal income tax

1973—U.S. Navy shuts down Quonset Point Naval Air Station

1978—A blizzard in February shuts down activity all over the state

1986—State constitutional convention is held

1989—The oil tanker *World Prodigy* runs aground, spilling thousands of gallons of oil in Narragansett Bay

1990—A banking crisis forces Governor Bruce Sundlun to shut down more than half of the state's banks and credit unions just hours after his inauguration on New Year's Day

IMPORTANT PEOPLE

WILLIAM ANDERS

William Alison (Bill) Anders (1933-   ), pilot, astronaut, executive; set several world flight records; as an astronaut (1963-69), was a crew member of *Apollo 8*, the first manned spacecraft to circle the moon; vice president of the Providence conglomerate Textron, Inc. (1954-89)

Leonard Bacon (1887-1954), poet; made his home in Peace Dale; known for his humorous, satirical verses on modern social problems; awarded the 1941 Pulitzer Prize in poetry for his collection *Sunderland Capture and Other Poems*; taught English at the University of California (1910-23)

John Brown (1736-1803), born in Providence; shipping merchant; wealthiest member of a prominent Providence mercantile family that included his brothers Joseph, Moses, and Nicholas; made his first fortune through slave trading and privateering; during the Revolutionary War, supplied clothing and munitions to the Continental army; his magnificent, fourteen-room house, designed by his brother Joseph, is now an important historic site on Providence's East Side

JOHN CARTER BROWN III

John Carter Brown (1797-1874), born in Providence; bibliophile, philanthropist; grandson of Nicholas Brown; his extensive collection of books on early America, which he donated to Brown University, became the renowned John Carter Brown Library

John Carter Brown III (1934-   ), born in Providence; curator; great-grandson of John Carter Brown; director of National Gallery of Art in Washington, D.C. (1969-   ); chairman of the U.S. Commission of Fine Arts; writer and director of the film *The American Vision* (1965)

JOSEPH BROWN

Joseph Brown (1733-1785), born in Providence; engineer, architect; designed Providence's First Baptist Meeting House (1775) and his brother John's house in Providence, considered two of the finest examples of colonial architecture in the country

NICHOLAS BROWN

AMBROSE BURNSIDE

GEORGE M. COHAN

EDDIE DOWLING

Moses Brown (1738-1836), born in Providence; merchant, manufacturer, abolitionist; his efforts led to the abolition of slavery in Rhode Island; launched the cotton manufacturing industry in America when, with the help of Samuel Slater, he built, in Pawtucket, the first textile mill in the U.S. to manufacture cotton thread using waterpower (1790)

Nicholas Brown (1729-1791), born in Providence; merchant; guided the family businesses, which included slave trading, distilling rum, making spermaceti candles, and producing iron and iron products; was influential in establishing Rhode Island College and ensuring that it was located in Providence; because of his endowment to the college, it was renamed Brown University in his honor; was instrumental in convincing Rhode Island to ratify the U.S. Constitution

Ambrose Everett Burnside (1824-1881), soldier, politician; commanded the Army of the Potomac in the U.S. Civil War; three-term governor of Rhode Island (1866-69); U.S. senator (1875-81)

Ruth Ann Buzzi (1936-   ), born in Westerly; actress, comedienne; acted in the Broadway production of *Sweet Charity* and several New York stage plays; appeared in numerous network television shows, including "Laugh-In"

George Michael Cohan (1878-1942), born in Providence; composer, singer, producer, actor, songwriter, playwright; considered to be the father of musical comedy in America; changed the trend in American musicals from foreign to American settings; for his patriotic World War I song "Over There," became the first composer to be awarded the Congressional Medal of Honor; songs include "Yankee Doodle Dandy," "You're a Grand Old Flag," and "Give My Regards to Broadway"

Leon N. Cooper (1930-   ), physicist, educator; with two other recipients, received 1972 Nobel Prize in physics; author of many articles for scientific journals; Brown University faculty member (1958-   )

Thomas Wilson Dorr (1805-1854), politician, social activist; in what was known as the "Dorr Rebellion," led an uprising against the Rhode Island state government to reform the state constitution, extend voting rights, and reapportion the legislature; major draftsman of the 1841 "People's Constitution"

Eddie Dowling (1894-1976), born Joseph Nelson Goucher in Woonsocket; theatrical producer, director, actor; began as a vaudeville performer with his wife, Ray Dooley; moved up from singing and dancing to producing plays; won New York Drama Critics Circle awards for four of his productions

Nelson Eddy (1901-1967), born in Providence; concert, opera, and radio singer; film actor; starred with Jeanette MacDonald in such films as *Sweethearts* and *Rose Marie*

Jabez Gorham (1792-1869), silversmith; born in Providence; father of Rhode Island's silverware industry; founder of Gorham Manufacturing Co., which became the largest producer of sterling silver in the world

Theodore Francis Green (1867-1966), born in Providence; businessman, politician; as Democratic governor of Rhode Island (1933-37), reformed state government offices and instituted social and economic reforms; as U.S. senator (1936-60), was the oldest person ever to serve in Congress; chaired the Senate Foreign Relations Committee (1957-59)

Nathanael Greene (1742-1786), born in Warwick; military leader; was second in command under General George Washington during the American Revolution; served in the Siege of Boston, the Battle of Long Island, and the Battle of Monmouth; commanded the Continental army's southern forces

Peter Harrison (1716-1775), merchant, architect; moved to Newport in 1740 and became involved in agriculture and shipping; most noted architect of mid-eighteenth-century America; using the Georgian architectural style, he designed Newport's Redwood Library, Brick Market, and Touro Synagogue

John Milton Hay (1838-1905), statesman; graduate of Brown University; private secretary to President Abraham Lincoln (1861-65); U. S. ambassador to Great Britain (1897-98); as U.S. secretary of state (1898-1905), helped formulate America's Open Door Policy toward China; Brown University's John Hay Library, named for him, houses the 11,000-item McLellan Lincoln Collection

Esek Hopkins (1718-1802), born near North Scituate; naval officer and seaman; first commander-in-chief of the Continental navy during the American Revolution; privateer during the Seven Year's War

Stephen Hopkins (1707-1785), born in Providence; patriot, politician; Rhode Island judge (1739-55) and legislator; governor of Rhode Island colony (1755, 1756, 1758-61, 1763, 1764, 1767); member of Continental Congress (1774-80); signed the Declaration of Independence; helped found *Providence Gazette & Coventry Journal*

Julia Ward Howe (1819-1910), reformer, writer, poet; lived in Portsmouth and Newport; best known for writing the text of "The Battle Hymn of the Republic"; in her later years worked for the abolition of slavery, women's rights, and other causes; published verses, travel sketches, and social criticisms; died in Newport

NELSON EDDY

NATHANAEL GREENE

JOHN HAY

JULIA WARD HOWE

JOHN LA FARGE

NAP LAJOIE

IRVING R. LEVINE

HORACE MANN

Anne Hutchinson (1591-1643), religious leader; advocate of religious freedom; helped establish the settlement of Portsmouth on Aquidneck Island in 1638

Edward Benjamin Koren (1935-   ), cartoonist, illustrator, author, educator; member of the art faculty at Brown University (1964-76); his cartoons have appeared in the *New Yorker, Time, Newsweek, Nation, Fortune, New York Times,* and many other publications

Christopher Grant La Farge (1862-1938), born in Newport; architect; specialized in designing churches; his architectural firm designed the interior of St. Paul the Apostle Church in New York City and many others

John La Farge (1835-1910), artist, writer; made his home in Newport; was influenced by the British Pre-Raphaelite style; painted murals and panels in Boston and New York City churches; father of Christopher La Farge

Oliver Hazard Perry La Farge (1901-1963), anthropologist, novelist; son of Christopher La Farge; won 1930 Pulitzer Prize for his first novel, *Laughing Boy;* lived in South County; published numerous novels and anthropological works on American Indian life

Napoleon (Nap) Lajoie (1875-1959), born in Woonsocket; baseball player; in his 1901 season with the Philadelphia Athletics, hit the highest season batting average (.422) in American League history; elected to the Baseball Hall of Fame (1937)

Irving Raskin Levine (1922-   ), born in Pawtucket; news commentator, writer; as an NBC correspondent, served in Korea, Moscow, Rome, London, and other major cities; author of several books, including *Main Street, U.S.S.R.* (1959)

Aaron Lopez (1731-1782), whaling, fishing, and candlemaking merchant; pioneered the manufacture of spermaceti candles from whale by-products; lost much of his wealth during the American Revolution; donated candelabra to Newport's Touro Synagogue

Howard Phillips (H. P.) Lovecraft (1890-1937), born in Providence; writer; his bizarre novels and short stories create a mythical world of superhuman creatures who interact with human beings

Horace Mann (1796-1859), lawyer, politician, educator; known as the father of American public education for his lifelong advocacy of publicly supported, nonsectarian education; graduated as valedictorian from Brown University (1819), where he also taught for a year; first head of Massachusetts's state board of education (1837-48); U.S. representative from Massachusetts (1848-53); president of coeducational, racially integrated Antioch College in Yellow Springs, Ohio (1853-59)

Edwin O'Connor (1918-1968), born in Providence; novelist; received 1962 Pulitzer Prize in fiction for his novel *The Edge of Sadness*, which traces three generations of an American family; other novels include *The Last Hurrah, I Was Dancing,* and *All in the Family*

Matthew Calbraith Perry (1794-1858), born in Newport; naval officer; fought in the War of 1812 and in the Mexican War (1847); as commander of America's East Indian Squadron, led U.S. mission to Japan in 1853 to open diplomatic and trade relations with that nation

OLIVER HAZARD PERRY

Oliver Hazard Perry (1785-1819), born in South Kingstown; naval officer; brother of Matthew Calbraith Perry; began working aboard ships at age fourteen; commanded a fleet of ships in the Great Lakes during the War of 1812; after his heroic victory in the Battle of Lake Erie, issued his now-famous report, "We have met the enemy and they are ours"

Samuel Slater (1768-1835), manufacturer; known as the father of the American textile industry, he built America's first waterpowered cotton-spinning machine in Pawtucket by reconstructing from memory the British Arkwright textile machinery

SAMUEL SLATER

Gilbert Stuart (1755-1828), born in North Kingstown; portrait artist; painted portraits of noted people of his day, including the first five presidents of the United States; best known for painting George Washington, of whom he made three portraits: a bust, a full-length portrait, and an unfinished head portrait, which now appears on U.S. one-dollar bills

GILBERT STUART

Abraham Touro (1777?-1822), born in Newport; merchant, philanthropist; prominent citizen and merchant shipper of Boston, Massachusetts; his $10,000 gift for the care and preservation of Newport's synagogue and cemetery, called the Touro Jewish Synagogue Fund, gave Touro Synagogue its name

Judah Touro (1775-1854), born in Newport; merchant, philanthropist; brother of Abraham Touro; settled in New Orleans, where he invested in shipping and real estate; fought and was wounded in the War of 1812; donated large amounts of money to Jewish and Christian charities

Roger Williams (1603?-1683), clergyman, colonial leader; regarded as the founder of Rhode Island; founded Providence in 1636; maintained friendly relations with the Indians of the region; first president of Rhode Island colony after it was chartered in 1644; known as an advocate of religious tolerance and democracy; wrote a book about Indian language, *A Key into the Language of America*; put forth his principles on religious freedom in *The Bloudy Tenent of Persecution*

ROGER WILLIAMS

GOVERNORS

Nicholas Cooke	1775-1778	Royal C. Taft	1888-1889
William Greene	1778-1786	Herbert W. Ladd	1889-1890
John Collins	1786-1790	John W. Davis	1890-1891
Arthur Fenner	1790-1805	Herbert W. Ladd	1891-1892
Henry Smith	1805	D. Russell Brown	1892-1895
Isaac Wilbur	1806-1807	Charles W. Lippitt	1895-1897
James Fenner	1807-1811	Elisha Dyer	1897-1900
William Jones	1811-1817	William Gregory	1900-1901
Nehemiah R. Knight	1817-1821	Charles D. Kimball	1901-1903
William C. Gibbs	1821-1824	Lucius F. C. Garvin	1903-1905
James Fenner	1824-1831	George H. Utter	1905-1907
Lemuel H. Arnold	1831-1833	James H. Higgins	1907-1909
John Brown Francis	1833-1838	Aram J. Pothier	1909-1915
William Sprague	1838-1839	R. Livingston Beeckman	1915-1921
Samuel Ward King	1840-1843	Emery J. San Souci	1921-1923
James Fenner	1843-1845	William S. Flynn	1923-1925
Charles Jackson	1845-1846	Aram J. Pothier	1925-1928
Byron Diman	1846-1847	Norman S. Case	1928-1933
Elisha Harris	1847-1849	Theodore F. Green	1933-1937
Henry B. Anthony	1849-1851	Robert E. Quinn	1937-1939
Philip Allen	1851-1853	William H. Vanderbilt	1939-1941
Francis M. Dimond	1853-1854	J. Howard McGrath	1941-1945
William W. Hoppin	1854-1857	John O. Pastore	1945-1950
Elisha Dyer	1857-1859	John S. McKiernan	1950-1951
Thomas G. Turner	1859-1860	Dennis J. Roberts	1951-1959
William Sprague	1860-1863	Christopher Del Sesto	1959-1961
William C. Cozzens	1863	John A. Notte, Jr.	1961-1963
James Y. Smith	1863-1866	John H. Chafee	1963-1969
Ambrose E. Burnside	1866-1869	Frank Licht	1969-1973
Seth Padelford	1869-1873	Philip W. Noel	1973-1977
Henry Howard	1873-1875	J. Joseph Garrahy	1977-1985
Henry Lippitt	1875-1877	Edward D. DiPrete	1985-1991
Charles C. Van Zandt	1877-1880	Bruce Sundlun	1991-
Alfred H. Littlefield	1880-1883		
Augustus O. Bourn	1883-1885		
George P. Wetmore	1885-1887		
John W. Davis	1887-1888		

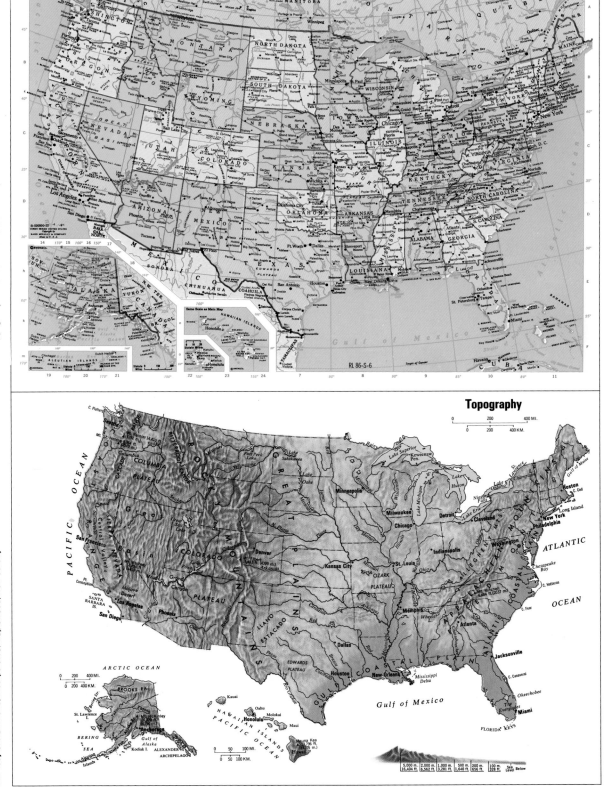

© Copyright by RAND MCNALLY & COMPANY, R.L. 89-S-82

Courtesy of Hammond, Incorporated, Maplewood, New Jersey

Topography

MAP KEY

Abbott Run	B4	Green Fall River	F2	Providence River	C5
		Greenville	C3	Prudence Island	E5
Adamsville	E6	Greenwich Bay	D4	Quicksand Pond	E6
Albion	B4	Hamilton	E4	Quidnessett	E4
Allenton	E4	Harmony	B3	Quidnick	D3
Alton	F2	Harris	D3	Quidnick Reservoir	D2
Anthony	D3	Harrisville	B2	Quinnville	B4
Arcadia	E2	Haversham	G2	Quonochontaug Pond	G2
Arkwright	D3	Hog Island	D5	Rhode Island (Aquidneck Island)	E5
Arnold Mills	B4	Hope	D3	Rhode Island Sound	F5
Arnold Mills Reservoir	B4	Hope Island	E5	Rockville	E1
Ashaway	F1	Hope Valley	E2	Sachuest Point	F6
Ashton	B4	Hopkinton	F1	Sakonnet Point	F6
Avondale	G1	Indian Lake Shores	F4	Sakonnet River	E6
Bald Hill	D2	Island Park	E6	Sandy Point	h7
Barden Reservoir	C2	Jackson	D3	Saunderstown	E4
Barrington	D5	Jamestown	F5	Saundersville	C3
Beaver River	E2	Jerimoth Hill	C1	Saylesville	B4
Beavertail Point	F4	Johnston	C4	Scituate Reservoir	C3
Belleville	E4	Kenyon	F2	Seekonk River	C4
Berkeley	B4	Kingston	F3	Shannock	F2
Blackstone River	B4	La Fayette	E4	Shore Acres	E4
Block Island	h7	Lippitt Estate	B4	Slatersville	A3
Block Island Sound	G2	Little Compton	E6	Slocum	E3
Bowdish Reservoir	B1	Lonsdale	B4	Smith and Sayles Reservoir	B2
Bradford	F2	Manville	B4	South Foster	C2
Branch Village	B3	Mapleville	B2	South Hopkinton	F1
Brenton Point	F5	Middletown	E5	Southwest Point	h7
Bristol	D5	Mohegan	B2	Spragueville	B3
Bristol Ferry	D5	Moosup River	C1	Stafford Pond	D6
Carolina	F2	Moosup Valley	D1	Summit	D2
Central Falls	B4	Moswansicut Pond	C3	Tarkiln	B3
Chapman Pond	F1	Mount Hope Bay	D6	Tenmile River	B5
Charlestown	F2	Mount View	D4	The Hummocks	D6
Chepachet	B2	Napatree Point	G1	Tiogue Lake	D3
Chepachet River	B2	Narragansett	F4	Tiverton	D6
Chipuxet River	F3	Narragansett Bay	E5	Tiverton Four Corners	E6
Clayville	C2	Nasonville	B3	Union Village	B3
Coasters Harbor Island	E5	Newport	F5	Usquepaug	F3
Conanicut Island	E5	Ninigret Pond	G2	Valley Falls	B4
Conimicut Point	D5	Nonquit Pond	E6	Wakefield	F3
Coventry	D3	North Kingstown	E4	Wallum Lake	A1
Cranston	C4	North Providence	C4	Warren	D5
Cumberland Hill	B4	North Scituate	C3	Warwick	D4
Davisville	E4	Oakland	B2	Watch Hill	G1
Diamond Hill	B4	Pascoag	B2	Watchaug Pond	F2
Diamond Hill Reservoir	A4	Patience Island	D5	Waterman Reservoir	B3
Dunns Corners	G1	Pawcatuck River	G1	Weekapaug	G1
Dutch Island	F4	Pawtucket	C4	West Barrington	C5
East Greenwich	D4	Pawtuxet River	D3	West Glocester	B1
East Matunuck	F3	Peace Dale	F3	West Kingston	F3
East Providence	C4	Perryville	F3	West Warwick	D3
Esmond	B4	Plum Beach	E4	Westconnaug Reservoir	C2
Exeter	E3	Plum Point	E4	Westerly	F1
Flat River Reservoir	D3	Point Judith	G4	White Rock	E1
Forestdale	B3	Point Judith Pond	F4	Wincheck Pond	E1
Foster	C2	Ponaganset Reservoir	B2	Wood River	F2
Galilee	F3	Ponaganset River	C2	Woonsocket	A3
Glendale	B2	Portsmouth	E6	Woonsocket Reservoir	B3
Great Salt Pond	h7	Potter Hill	F1	Worden Pond	F3
Great Swamp	F3	Primrose	B3	Wyoming	E2
		Providence	C4	Yorktown Manor	C3

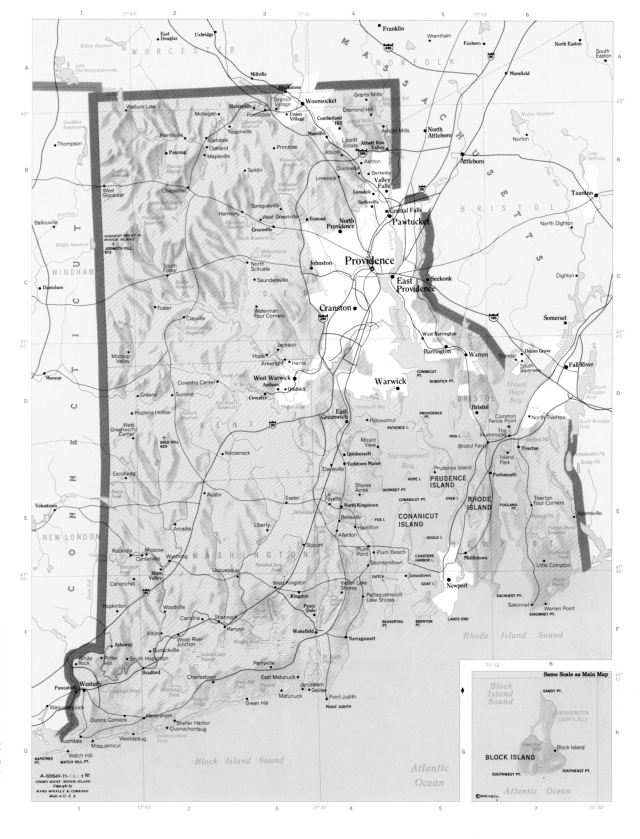

Copyright by RAND McNALLY, R.L. 89-S-221

MASSACHUSETTS

WORCESTER

NORFOLK

BRISTOL

WINDHAM

PROVIDENCE

CONNECTICUT

KENT

NEW LONDON

WASHINGTON

BRISTOL

NEWPORT

Mount
Hope
Bay

Narragansett
Bay

PRUDENCE
ISLAND

CONANICUT
ISLAND

RHODE
ISLAND

Rhode   Island   Sound

Block Island Sound

Atlantic
Ocean

Franklin
Wrentham
Foxboro
North Easton
South Easton
East Douglas
Uxbridge
Mansfield
Millville
Norton
North Attleboro
Grants Mills
Woonsocket
Diamond Hill
Cumberland Hill
Arnold Mills
North Attleboro
Attleboro
North Dighton
Taunton
Dighton
Somerset
Fall River

Providence
Pawtucket
Central Falls
East Providence
Seekonk
Cranston
Warwick

HIGHEST POINT IN RHODE ISLAND
JERIMOTH HILL 812

BALD HILL 629

Same Scale as Main Map

Block
Island
Sound

SANDY PT.

(WASHINGTON
COUNTY, R.I.)

BLOCK ISLAND

Block Island

SOUTHWEST PT.

SOUTHEAST PT.

Atlantic
Ocean

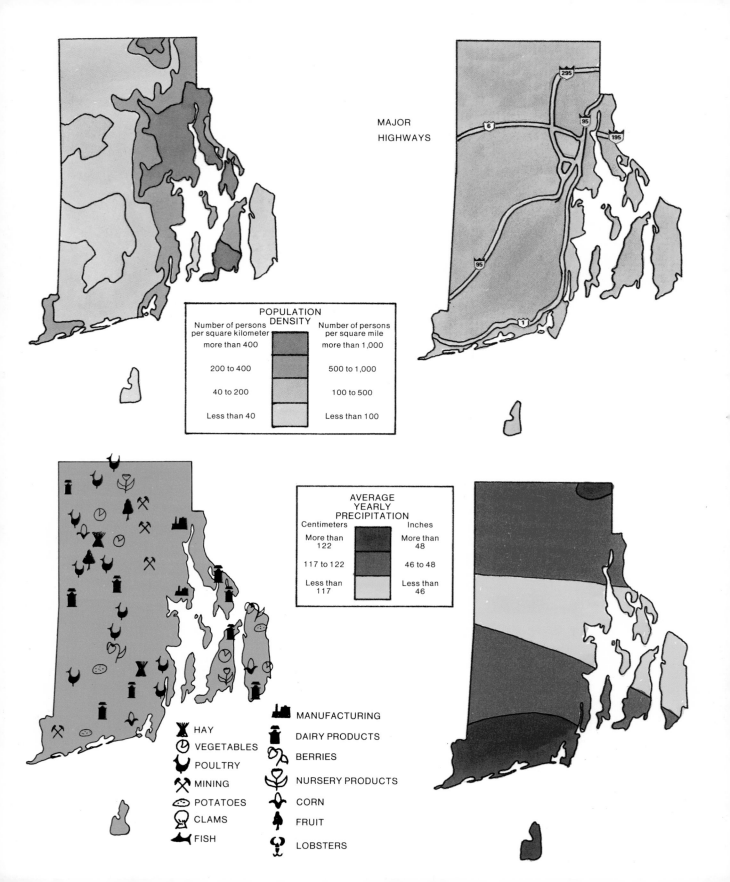

MAJOR HIGHWAYS

POPULATION DENSITY

Number of persons per square kilometer	Number of persons per square mile
more than 400	more than 1,000
200 to 400	500 to 1,000
40 to 200	100 to 500
Less than 40	Less than 100

AVERAGE YEARLY PRECIPITATION

Centimeters	Inches
More than 122	More than 48
117 to 122	46 to 48
Less than 117	Less than 46

HAY
VEGETABLES
POULTRY
MINING
POTATOES
CLAMS
FISH

MANUFACTURING
DAIRY PRODUCTS
BERRIES
NURSERY PRODUCTS
CORN
FRUIT
LOBSTERS

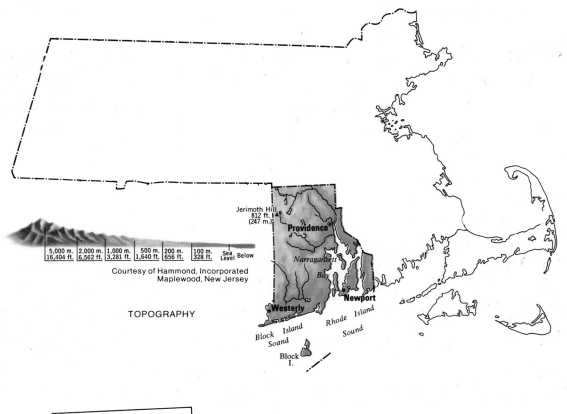

5,000 m. | 2,000 m. | 1,000 m. | 500 m. | 200 m. | 100 m. | Sea | Below
16,404 ft. | 6,562 ft. | 3,281 ft. | 1,640 ft. | 656 ft. | 328 ft. | Level |

Courtesy of Hammond, Incorporated
Maplewood, New Jersey

Jerimoth Hill
812 ft.
(247 m.)

Providence

Narragansett
Bay

Newport

Westerly

Rhode Island
Sound

Block Island
Sound

Block
I.

TOPOGRAPHY

PROVIDENCE

PROVIDENCE ⊕

KENT

East Greenwich •

BRISTOL

Bristol
•

NEWPORT

WASHINGTON

West Kingston •

• Newport

COUNTIES

(NEWPORT CO)

Wickford, in Washington County

INDEX

Page numbers that appear in boldface type indicate illustrations

138

140

Fourth of July parade in Bristol

Picture Identifications

Front Cover: Ocean Drive in Newport
Back Cover: Providence at dusk
Pages 2-3: Sakonnet Point, Sakonnet
Page 6: Statue of the Independent Man while it was temporarily on display inside Rhode Island's State House
Pages 8-9: Block Island Lighthouse, Block Island
Pages 18-19: Montage of Rhode Island residents
Page 26: Adriaen Block, the explorer for whom Block Island is named, building a boat with his men
Pages 38-39: A lithograph depicting Newport in 1730
Pages 52-53: Young girls employed at a Rhode Island textile mill in the early 1900s
Page 62: The Rhode Island State House
Pages 76-77: The South County Hot Air Balloon Festival
Pages 90-91: Historic houses along Thomas Street in Providence
Page 108: Montage of state symbols including the state tree (red maple), state flag, state bird (Rhode Island Red chicken), state mineral (bowenite) and state shell (quahog)

Picture Acknowledgments

Front cover, © **Paul Darling**; 2-3, 4, 5, © **Jack Spratt**; 6, ©**Paul Darling**; 8-9, © George Goodwin/**SuperStock International**; 11, ©**Kathryn Whitney**; 12, © **Boyd Norton**; 15 (left), © **Jack Spratt**; 15 (right), © **John DeWaele**; 16 (left), © **Paul Darling**; 16 (right), © **Arthur Swoger**; 17 (two pictures), © **Paul Darling**; 18 (top left), © **Jack Spratt**; 18 (top right, bottom left, bottom right), © **Paul Darling**; 19 (top left, bottom left), © **Jack Spratt**; 19 (top right), © **Jeff Greenberg**; 19 (middle left, bottom right), © **Paul Darling**; 21, © **Mary Ann Brockman**; 22, 24 (left), © **Paul Darling**; 24 (right), 25, © **Jack Spratt**; 26, **North Wind Picture Archives**; 28, **Museum of Art, Rhode Island School of Design; Gift of Mr. Robert Winthrop**; 31 (left), **Historical Pictures Service, Chicago**; 31 (right), 32, **The Rhode Island Historical Society**; 35, © **Joseph A. DiChello, Jr.**; 37, **The Rhode Island Historical Society**; 38-39, **Newport Historical Society**; 41 (two pictures), 43, 44, 47, **The Rhode Island Historical Society**; 48 (left), © Clark/**Photri**; 48 (right), 49, **The Rhode Island Historical Society**; 50, **North Wind Picture Archives**; 51, © Steve Solum / **Third Coast Stock Source**; 52-53, 55, **Slater Mill Historic Site**; 56, © **Mary Ann Brockman**; 59, **AP/Wide World Photos**; 61, © **John DeWaele**; 62, © David Forbert/**Shostal/SuperStock**; 66, © **Mary Ann Brockman**; 67, © David Forbert/**Shostal/ SuperStock**; 69, **Rhode Island Department of Economic Development**; 70, © **Jeff Greenberg**; 71 © **Paul Darling**; 72 (left), © **Jack Spratt**; 72 (right), © **Frank W. Mantlik**; 73, © **John DeWaele**; 74, © **Ken Laffal/Root Resources**; 76-77, 79, © **Jack Spratt**; 80 (left), © **Ken Laffal/Root Resources**; 80 (right), **Rhode Island Department of Economic Development**; 82, © **Mary Ann Brockman**; 85 (left), © **Joseph A. DiChello**; 85 (right), © **Paul Darling**; 86, © **Joseph A. DiChello**; 87, © **Paul Darling**; 88, (left), © **Doris DeWitt/TSW-Click/Chicago Ltd.**; 88 (right), © **Paul Darling**; 90-91, © David Forbert/**Shostal/SuperStock**; 93, © **Paul Darling**; 93 (map), **Len W. Meents**; 94, © **John DeWaele**; 96, © **Gene Ahrens/SuperStock International**; 97 (left), © David Forbert/**Shostal/SuperStock**; 97 (right), © **Bryan Hemphill/Root Resources**; 98 (left), © **Paul Darling**; 98 (right), David Forbert/**Shostal/ SuperStock**; 100 (top left), © **Ken Laffal/Root Resources**; 100 (top right, bottom left), © **Paul Darling**; 100 (bottom right), © **Judy Colbert**; 103, © George Goodwin/**SuperStock International**; 103 (map), **Len W. Meents**; 104, © **Ken Laffal/Root Resources**; 105, **Photri**; 107, © **John DeWaele**; 108 (tree, bird), **Shostal/SuperStock**; 108 (shell), © **Paul Darling**; 108 (mineral), **Rhode Island Department of Economic Development**; 108 (flag), **courtesy of Flag Research Center, Winchester, Massachusetts 01890**; 111, © **Jack Spratt**; 112, © **Frank W. Mantlik**; 117, © **Ken Laffal/Root Resources**; 118, **Shostal/ SuperStock**; 120, 121, © **Paul Darling**; 123, © David Forbert/ **Shostal/SuperStock**; 127 (Anders), **AP/ Wide World Photos**; 127 (John Carter Brown III), **Bettmann Newsphotos**; 127 (Joseph Brown), 128 (Nicholas Brown), **North Wind Picture Archives**; 128 (Burnside, Cohan, Dowling), 129 (Eddy, Greene), **AP/Wide World Photos**; 129 (Hay), **Historical Pictures Service Chicago**; 129 (Howe), 130 (La Farge), **North Wind Picture Archives**; 130 (Lajoie, Levine), **AP/Wide World Photos**; 130 (Mann), **Historical Pictures Service, Chicago**; 131 (Perry, Stuart), **North Wind Picture Archives**; 131 (Slater, Williams), **Historical Pictures Service, Chicago**; 132, **AP/Wide World Photos**; 136 (maps), **Len W. Meents**; 138, 141, © **Jack Spratt**; back cover, © **Mary Ann Brockman**

About the Author

Ann Heinrichs is a free-lance writer and editor living in Chicago. She has worked for such educational publishers as Encyclopaedia Britannica, World Book Encyclopedia, and Science Research Associates. As a music critic and feature writer, her articles have appeared in various publications. She is the author of a number of books, including several in the *America the Beautiful* series.